主编／胡霞 刘涛 黄雨晴
编委／王靖雯 周城晨 游佳
吴洁 魏敏 陈俊名 Calvin McDonald
钟佩好 吴诗然 孙伊然 周丹
钟远波

理解与融通
——树德中学国际理解课程经典课案集

四川大学出版社
SICHUAN UNIVERSITY PRESS

项目策划：唐　飞
责任编辑：唐　飞
特邀编辑：王心怡
责任校对：孙明丽
封面设计：墨创文化
责任印制：王　炜

图书在版编目（CIP）数据

理解与融通：树德中学国际理解课程经典课案集／胡霞，刘涛，黄雨晴主编．— 成都：四川大学出版社，2022.3
ISBN 978-7-5690-5393-7

Ⅰ．①理… Ⅱ．①胡… ②刘… ③黄… Ⅲ．①国情教育—教案（教育）—中学 Ⅳ．① G633.202

中国版本图书馆CIP数据核字（2022）第 039831 号

书名　理解与融通——树德中学国际理解课程经典课案集
LIJIE YU RONGTONG—SHUDEZHONGXUE GUOJI LIJIE KECHENG JINGDIAN KE'ANJI

主　　编	胡　霞　刘　涛　黄雨晴
出　　版	四川大学出版社
地　　址	成都市一环路南一段24号（610065）
发　　行	四川大学出版社
书　　号	ISBN 978-7-5690-5393-7
印前制作	四川胜翔数码印务设计有限公司
印　　刷	郫县犀浦印刷厂
成品尺寸	170mm×240mm
印　　张	10.5
字　　数	198千字
版　　次	2022年3月第1版
印　　次	2022年3月第1次印刷
定　　价	50.00元

◆ 版权所有 ◆ 侵权必究 ◆

◆ 读者邮购本书，请与本社发行科联系。
　电话：(028)85408408/(028)85401670/
　(028)86408023　邮政编码：610065
◆ 本社图书如有印装质量问题，请寄回出版社调换。
◆ 网址：http://press.scu.edu.cn

四川大学出版社
微信公众号

文化理解视野下的国际理解教育新使命

李江源

成都是地方政府创办官办学校较早的地区之一,素有尊师重教、广纳英才、敢为天下先的传统。"成都教育"不断提高教育国际化水平,加强中外人文教育交流。树德中学不断加强普通高中国际理解教育课程建设,培养树德学子的国际交流能力和国际竞争能力,让树德学子通过对世界的认识来了解自己和他人,引导树德学子树立人类共同价值观。同时,树德中学还大胆探索,打造树德中学中外人文教育交流品牌,增强树德中学的国际吸引力、影响力、竞争力与教育话语权。

一、在全球化视野下开启"成都教育"全新的理论境界和理论视野

在全球化时代,我们应以开放的视野理解"成都教育",同时应以开放的视野发展"成都教育"。在教育国际化进程中,"成都教育"牢牢坚持以下"铁律"。

一是坚持合作共赢理念,把握成都与其他国家或地区教育合作与交流的正确方向。合作共赢理念是成都与其他国家或地区进行教育合作与交流的灵魂。在一个相互依赖的世界里,成都与其他国家或地区的教育合作与交流不是"你死我活"的竞争,不是"你输我赢"的博弈。相互依赖是教育合作与交流的基础,"成都教育"的发展与进步就是其他国家或地区教育的发展与进步,其他

国家或地区教育的发展与进步也是"成都教育"的发展与进步。其他国家或地区教育的发展与进步是"成都教育"的"利好","成都教育"的发展与进步是其他国家或地区教育的机遇。"现代国家,即使只考虑它们自身的利益,也不能不发觉,增强国家之间的合作和更自由地、更有组织地交换文献和经验,将有助于它们在自己的事业上取得更廉价和更迅速的进步。"① 成都与其他国家或地区都应超越教育制度差异,摒弃零和思维,积极实践同舟共济、合作共赢的理念,相互包容、良性竞争,共享教育革新经验,共担教育发展风险。

二是做大教育合作与交流"蛋糕",夯实成都与其他国家或地区教育合作与交流的基础。在"公园城市"理念引领下,成都与其他国家或地区进行教育合作与交流的契合点、共同点日渐增多,深化教育合作面临新机遇。成都对"城乡教育一体化"的实践,对教育公平正义的探索,将为其他国家或地区推进城乡教育均衡发展提供经验,为其他国家或地区的学者提供鲜活的研究范本,为世界教育宝库增添新素材。其他国家或地区的先进教育理念、先进教育管理经验等,也将为"成都教育"的发展注入新的动力。"海纳百川,有容乃大",成都与其他国家或地区在教育合作与交流过程中,不断创新教育合作与交流形式,拓展教育合作领域,促进了双方或多方教育的发展与进步。

三是加强教育合作与教育交流,构筑成都与其他国家或地区教育合作与交流的精神纽带。"国之交在于民相亲,民相亲在于心相通。"成都与其他国家或地区教育合作与交流的加强,不仅需要教育项目、科研项目作为合作的载体,而且需要人民的理解和互信作为精神保障,需要国际理解教育作为支撑。有了文明的对话,才会有心灵的交流,才会达到"心有灵犀一点通"的境界。由交流而理解,由理解而包容,由包容而互信,不断增强同舟共济、合作共赢意识。成都应更加积极地推进与其他国家或地区社会各界的交流,加强教育领域的合作,用教育交流乃至民间交流培植合作与交流的社会基础和民意基础,用教育交流架起人民相互了解和友谊的桥梁。

四是妥善管控教育合作与交流过程中的分歧和摩擦,切实推进"成都教育"教育国际化的大发展。成都与其他国家或地区的教育文化、教育传统、教育制度、教育发展阶段乃至关注的教育问题不同,因此在一些教育问题上存在不同看法实属正常。随着教育合作与交流的增多,产生一些竞争和摩擦也在所难免。成都与其他国家或地区在教育合作与交流过程中都应相互尊重、相互理

---

① 联合国教科文组织国际教育发展委员会编著,华东师范大学比较教育研究所译:《学会生存——教育的今天和明天》,教育科学出版社,1996年版,第3页。

解、平等相待、互谅互让，善于"换位思考"，懂得"将心比心"与"同情性理解"，在坚持自身教育理念、维护自身教育制度等的同时倾听对方的质疑之声以及不同主张，通过对话与协商妥善解决分歧。对话与协商不仅能"使人们深入认识和了解差异性，同时也提供了一种途径，使人们都能尊重差异性"[①]。

在坚持以上"铁律"的同时，"成都教育"积极探索、大胆试验，寻求"本土化"与"国际化"的有机融合，并不断丰富"成都教育"的实践特色、理论特色、民族特色、本土特色和时代特色。这里所谓的"成都教育"，并非具有限制或限定的意义，并非限定成都只能关注"成都教育"在其发展过程中呈现的各种教育现象，解决"成都教育"在其发展过程中出现的各种问题，求解"成都教育"在其发展过程中涌现的各种困惑，而是使"成都教育"具有开放性的意义，表明成都能够依托厚重的中华民族传统文化优势、独特的本土文化优势以及教育理论优势和教育制度优势来解决人类共同面临的教育问题，解释人类共同存在的教育现象，并为发展中国家在城市化进程中如何确保教育公平提供参考，如何破解教育不公平提供解决之策。如是，"成都教育"的独立与自信使得成都在全球化背景下的教育理论境界和教育视野发生了根本性转变：从"朝朝不见日，岁岁不知春"的幽闭情怀转向"家事国事天下事，事事关心"的入世情怀；从"自说自话"的封闭性立场转向教育国际性话语权——"普通话"的开放立场；从"独善其身"的防御性姿态转向"兼济天下"的积极性姿态。发展起来的"成都教育"正逐渐成为世界教育发展的重要组成部分，成为世界教育共同体大家庭中的核心成员。在全球化场域中，"成都教育"的教育理论体系、教育制度体系、教育实践探索对于应对人类共同的教育发展问题、人类教育文明进步问题具有独特的优势。"成都教育"努力践行的教育公平、教育民主、教育和谐、城乡教育均衡发展、城乡教育一体化发展等教育理念，体现出一种特有的开放与包容，既倚仗其他国家或地区先进的教育理念、教育经验，又完全展现出"成都教育"参验本土教育生活的"精髓"，体悟本土教育现实的"道法"；既坚持全人类的共同教育价值与中华民族传统文化、成都本土文化的底蕴，又充分表达出"成都教育"在培育和践行人类共同追求的优秀教育价值方面具有的教育理论自信和教育制度自信。

---

① 埃利诺等著，郭少文译：《对话：变革之道》（译丛总序），教育科学出版社，2006年，第240页。

二、在实践中培育、在理论上阐释"成都教育"的教育理论自信和教育制度自信

"成都教育"是否能在国际社会、在世界性城市中确立自己的地位,发出自己的"声音",唱响自己的"主旋律",打造自己的教育品牌,提升自己的教育影响力,从根本上讲取决于以下三点:一是"成都教育"所确立的教育理论体系、教育制度体系、教育实践探索如何能够在推动经济社会发展,确保教育公平正义,提高教育质量,促进学生全面、自由、充分发展方面体现自己的发展优势?二是"成都教育"所确立的教育理论体系、教育制度体系、教育实践探索如何能够在学生价值观培育和全人类教育发展与进步方面体现自己的价值优势?三是"成都教育"所确立的教育理论体系、教育制度体系、教育实践探索如何能够在城市化进程中,确保人的权利、人的尊严和人的价值?要回答这三个问题,"成都教育"必须围绕参与教育全球化进程和建构"成都教育"的特色等来培育"自觉"和"自信"。

今天,深刻影响着全人类教育发展与进步的最重要的历史机制是全球化的逻辑,最强有力的动力机制是教育国际化的"国家实力"逻辑,最现实的推进机制是教育本土化与教育国际化相互依存的"人才竞争"逻辑。"成都教育"的教育理论和教育实践,首先要面对的是三大现实:一是"成都教育"的教育理论体系和教育制度的优越性应当体现为,在积极参与教育全球化、教育国际化进程的同时,对教育全球化、教育国际化的逻辑保持清醒的反思意识和批判精神。二是"成都教育"的教育理论体系和教育制度的优越性应当体现为,在积极推进教育国际化、借鉴国际上先进的教育理念和教育经验的前提下,批判和抑制教育全球化、教育国际化的逻辑所造成的各种不平等、不人道的消极后果。"从总体来看,全球化要求每个国家必须具备一些特殊的优势,只有这样才能参与世界经济关系的发展,全球化使发展的成功者和失败者之间的差距更加明显。全球化的另一个特征是……知识的差距将会进一步扩大,致使那些缺乏知识的国家与这方面的重要活动更加无缘。"[①] 三是"成都教育"的教育理论体系、教育制度设计与安排的优越性应当体现为,在最大限度地激励和保护

---

① 联合国教科文组织编,联合国教科文组织总部中文科译:《教育——财富蕴藏其中》,教育科学出版社,2014年,第6页。

教育国际化所要求的教育各层面、各领域的创新基础上，对教育全球化的"西化"本性和"文化殖民"加以有效的道德与价值约束，以及教育法律与教育制度约束。教育革新信息、教育理论体系、教育经验在世界范围内的自由流通，一方面改变了人们对教育的认识，另一方面其消极作用不容忽视。拥有教育革新信息、"先进"教育理念和教育经验的发达国家或私营集团正是因为掌握了这些信息系统而具有真正的文化和政治影响力。"少数国家几乎对全部文化产业的垄断及其产品在全世界广大公众中的日益广泛的传播，对各种文化特性具有很强的侵蚀作用。这种虚伪的'世界文化'，尽管非常单调而且内容往往极其贫乏，但并不会因此而不宣扬某些隐晦的价值观，而且还可能会使那些受到其影响的人产生一种失落感和失去特性的感觉。"①

只有"成都教育"的教育实践经验优势、教育理论优势、教育制度优势乃至教育价值优势在教育运行的各个层面上都扎实地培育起来、扩大开来，并且在教育实践经验上得以系统总结，在教育理论上得以清晰阐释，在教育制度上得以科学设计，在教育价值上得以合目的性论证，"成都教育"对教育公平的维护、教育制度的建设、教育民主与法治的建构、教育价值观的培育和提升、教育影响力与竞争力的扩大等，才能确立扎实的根基，才能达到"本立而道生"。如是，"成都教育"的教育理论自信和教育制度自信就会"水到渠成"。

三、国际理解的本质是文化理解和文明互鉴

2017 年发布的《中国学生核心素养》对国际理解素养的定义是："具有全球意识和开放的心态，了解人类文明进程和世界发展动态；能尊重世界多元文化的多样性和差异性，积极参与跨文化交流；关注人类面临的全球性挑战，理解人类命运共同体的内涵与价值。"换句话说，国际理解的关键是文化理解。

各国发展道路和文化的差异根源于文明路向的不同，不同的民族呈现出不同的文明景观。只有深刻理解本民族的文化并以尊重、包容、开放的心态对待世界多元文化，才能进行平等的文明对话，建立真正的国际理解。当然，东西方文化各有其源头，虽因地理环境、生产方式、历史发展差异等原因呈现出不同的发展面貌，但都为人类文明做出了重大贡献。每一种文化都有其独特的价

---

① 联合国教科文组织编，联合国教科文组织总部中文科译：《教育——财富蕴藏其中》，教育科学出版社，2014 年，第 7 页。

值,这种价值是与其特殊的环境相匹配的,不同种类的文明形态在价值上是平等、多元和相对的。因此,东西方文化理应相互交流和借鉴。

新时代国际理解教育必须自觉坚定文化自信,坚守中华文化立场,铸牢中华民族共同体意识,不断扩大中国教育在世界教育格局中的活跃度和影响力,在建设社会主义文化强国、实现中华民族伟大复兴中发挥强基固本的独特作用。坚守中华文化立场,推动中华优秀传统文化创造性转化、创新性发展。中华优秀传统文化是中华民族的精神命脉,培育了中华民族共同的情感和价值、共有的理想和精神,是最深厚的文化软实力。孔子、孟子、陶行知等的教育思想汇成的中国教育学长河,绵延着中华优秀传统文化的血脉,为中华民族提供了丰厚滋养,为世界文明贡献了华彩篇章。新时代中国教育要自觉运用马克思主义的立场、观点和方法,发掘中华优秀传统文化的当代价值,正确处理传统与现代、守正与创新的关系,既保持文化的民族性,赓续中华深厚文脉,又体现文化的时代性,融入当代文化资源,推进中华优秀传统文化与革命文化、社会主义先进文化源流相汇、浩荡前行。

自信展示真实、立体、全面的"中国教育""成都教育",增强中国学校在全球语境中的对话沟通能力,国际理解教育课程发挥着不可替代的作用。在新的征程上,国际理解教育课程建设围绕党和国家教育改革发展大局,充分发挥其在人文交流和民心相通方面的独特作用,讲好中国教育故事,传播中国教育声音,阐发中国教育精神,展现中国教育风貌;运用丰富多样的叙述话语、表现风格、艺术手法向世界展现发生在新时代中国大地上的教育奇迹,呈现新时代中国学校的风貌与魅力,展示中华文明的博大精深与当代价值;打造中国学校国际理解课程建设品牌,构建既具有本土化、特色化又充分考虑各国文化多样性、尊重各国文化习俗的跨文化课程体系;将中国学校国际理解课程建设"走出去"汇入中华文化"走出去"的洪流,以文载道、以文传声、以文化人,向世界阐释推介更多具有中国特色、体现中国精神、蕴藏中国智慧的优秀文化,努力塑造可信、可爱、可敬的"中国教育形象""成都教育品牌",赢得尊重、赢得认同,为实现中华民族伟大复兴创造有利的国际环境,为推动构建人类命运共同体作出树德中学的贡献。

四、普通高中国际理解课程经典案例的创造与启示

在成都这块中国教育改革开放的热土上,有一所致力于基础教育改革的学

校——树德中学。该校高举"聚焦国际理解课程建设"旗帜，十多年来，进行了一系列以"国际理解教育"为主线、以单元设计为切入口、富有特色的课程开发与课堂转型实践探索。

《理解与融通——树德中学国际理解课程经典课案集》就实现了课程整合。具体而言，第一，教学内容的整合。通过专题型学习实现教学内容的整合，如对中西茶文化、中西节日等专题问题展开学习。在围绕特定课题展开的学习过程中，教学完全基于学生的兴趣爱好，而并未忽视学科本质，也未打破学科框架。第二，学习方式的整合。通过从扩散到收束的多样的学习方式，实现了学习方式的变革。首先，围绕课题探讨而展开拓展性学习活动（取材、制作、调查、实验、演出）；其次，组织报告会（文献收集、讨论集会、信息交流）等收束活动。多样化的学习方式，让学生在主体性问题解决的场域中，展开制作、培育、体验、达成、观察、讨论、验证、发表、行动等活动。第三，学习场域的整合。国际理解课程建设不仅重视学生的兴趣与爱好，还充分发掘学校与社区的特色并将之相融合，以此拓展学生的学习资源，形成广泛的学生体验活动场所。还广泛运用校园以及社区相关设施与影响力，大大扩充了学生的学习资源，丰富了学生同社区乃至国内和国际各方面相关教育的交流。

目 录

课程目标与实施……………………………………………………（001）

探索世界篇

中西茶文化对比……………………………………………………（010）

从经济学角度分析茶馆的收益与成本……………………………（020）

韩国人口危机………………………………………………………（027）

中西节日对比研究…………………………………………………（038）

分辨视角篇

探索自己的价值观…………………………………………………（050）

性别思维定式

——赋能学生　主动学习…………………………………（064）

不同文化对于想象力的影响………………………………………（079）

多变量微积分在国内外的应用……………………………………（090）

沟通思想篇

文化身份认知………………………………………………………（100）

新加坡英语…………………………………………………………（108）

构建包容性的社会…………………………………………………（117）

宽窄巷子研学设计…………………………………………………（130）

采取行动篇

项目化学习之"财商与决策"………………………………………（140）

经济学思维…………………………………………………………（149）

课程目标与实施

当今世界全球化趋势已势不可挡，各国在各方面的相互依赖程度逐步加深。联合国教科文组织在1945年正式倡导"国际理解"的概念。什么是国际理解？国际理解是跨越国家和民族的互相理解，以相互尊重为基础，且"国际理解""合作""和平"应被视为一个不可分割的整体。

树德中学，秉承"树人先树德"，其树德广才的办学思想是对"树德"二字最好的诠释，即"成才要成人，树人先树德，树德以广才"，充分体现了"树德"和"广才"相辅相成，互为目的、途径、方法和保证。"树德"益智、"广才"积德，二者相得益彰。

这样的办学理念跟国际理解课程的概念有什么联系呢？"树德树人"中什么是"德"？什么是"人"？道德是社会意识形态之一，是人们共同生活及其行为的准则和规范。在当今全球化的背景下，我们认为"德"的标准不仅仅是形成标准的社会准则与规范，更重要的是要对其他国家或地区的社会行为规范和准则有认知和理解，对其他文化的行为准则进行批判性的思考。"树人"即对人的品质进行塑造。在全球化趋势下，作为学生首先需要认知自我，在自我的认知中找到自己的价值。

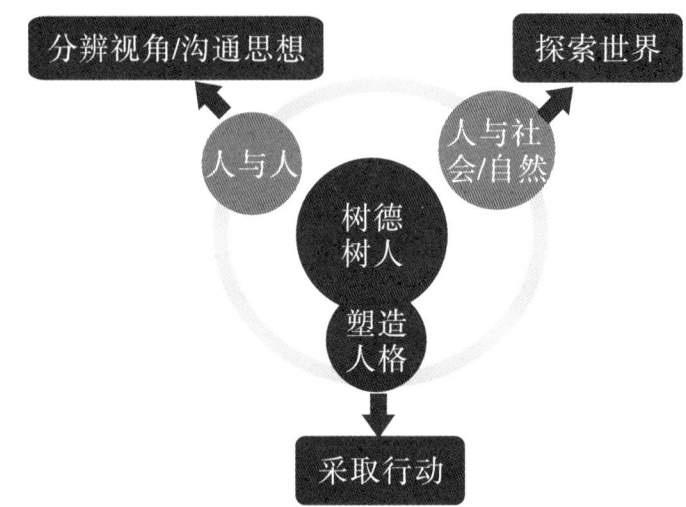

树德中学的国际理解课程目标融合了全球胜任力的教学目标。2018年,国际经合组织(OECD)在国际学生评估项目(PISA)对全球胜任力的解释中给出四个维度的能力:

(1) 能够分析具有当地、全球和跨文化重要意义的议题和形势。

(2) 能够理解与欣赏不同视角和世界观。

(3) 能够与不同国家、民族、宗教、社会、文化、性别的人建立良性互动。

(4) 能够并愿意为可持续发展和集体福祉采取建设性的行动。

另外,联合国教科文组织对国际理解的教学目标规定中有以下三个维度:

知识维度	态度和价值观维度	技能和能力维度
民族间的平等	自我尊重	批判思维
和平的维护	尊重别人	问题解决
人权	对生态关怀	合作
发展	致力于和平公正	想象力
环境	心胸开阔无偏见	自信
国际理解和文化遗产	换位思考和同情心	冲突解决
联合国系统	团结	宽容
		参与
		沟通能力

树德中学的国际理解课程目标结合 PISA 全球胜任力与国际理解的三个维度目标，制订了自己的国际理解课程教学目标：

（1）能够分析成都当地的文化议题，并且跟全球文化联系起来，进行分析、对比。

（2）能够了解周围人的视角、观点形成方式，了解不同的世界观是如何形成的，并且对不同的世界观进行批判性思考。

（3）能够对外宣传本土文化，与有不同文化背景的人建立互动。

（4）能够对自己感兴趣的话题进行深入研究，并且采取建设性的行动。

在实施过程中，树德中学有以下几个原则：

（1）课程涵盖内容广泛，从语言学科，到地理、历史、经济等学科的内容，不仅扩展学生的知识面，也补充了一些初高中缺乏的科目知识，或是将一些科目的知识进行了串联。

（2）课程的实施坚持 SAGE（Students Choice，学生选择；Authentic Experience，真实体验；Global Significance，全球意义；Exhibit to Real Audience，真实观众）原则：学生自主选择，真实体验。这也是全球胜任力的教学原则。学生能够对自己感兴趣的领域进行研究，塑造真实的任务并在真实环境中展示。话题要具有全球意义，以此培养世界公民素养。

（3）在教学阶段，我们实施构建主义原则，让学生在已知的认知领域通过教师的引导进行知识的构建。在实施过程中，每次课程都需要达成知识、认知、深度思考三个层次的目标。

（4）在课程教学中进行多维度评估，运用 AfL（Assessment for Learning，学习性评价）原则，对学生的知识、技能和态度进行评估。评估方式不限于测试，也会采用论文或文章写作、真实合作任务等多种评估方式。也可以针对不同学生的能力和天赋在多维度层面对学生的知识、技能和价值观进行测试。

课程的评估

树德中学国际部成立于 2002 年，国际教育经验丰富，硕果累累。树德中学国际部在 IB 课程（International Baccalaureate，国际文凭课程）教学方面一直位于西南领先、全国一流的位置。在国际理解课程的评估中也借用了 IB 课程的评估。

评估主要分为形成性评估与总结性评估。

1. 形成性评估

形成性评估主要基于平时课堂中学生的小组作业、口头报告等。让学生有真实的参与感是评估的重要原则。

有的学生参与制作网站，讨论全球议题：经济发展与环保的关系、社交媒体对外貌认识的影响等。学生把对全球议题的思考通过网站的方式向全世界展示，表达自己对议题的思考。

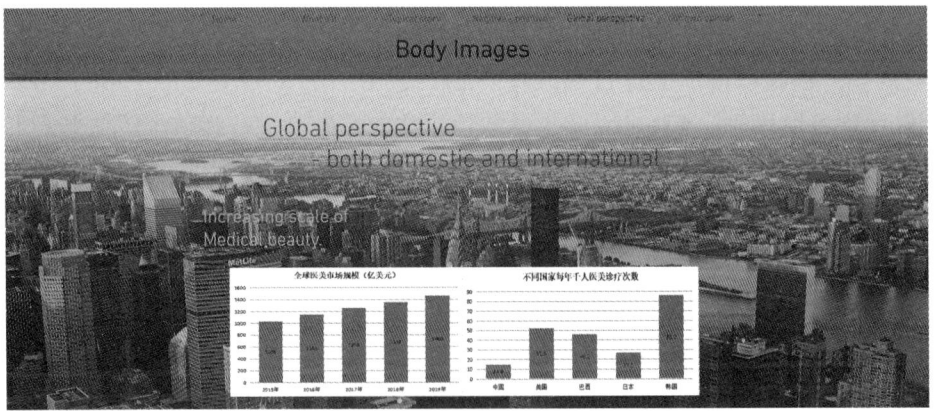

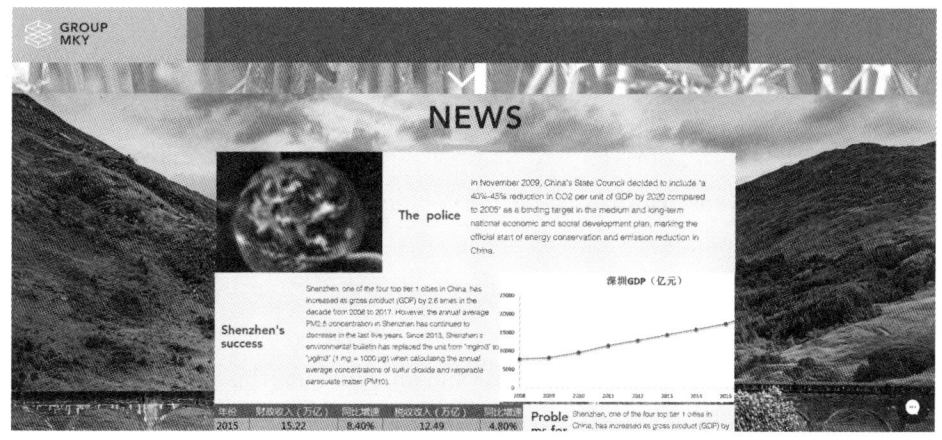

部分学生的网站作品

有的学生在学习了中西方艺术之后,自己创造艺术作品来展示文化与艺术的关系。例如,F同学创作的这幅现代版的《历代帝王图》结合中国唐朝时期的《历代帝王图》进行了改版,并联系西方艺术中的经典之作——达·芬奇的《最后的晚餐》,借鉴了《最后的晚餐》的餐桌结构。在餐桌上的不再是西方食物而是各种中国食物,还有世界各地的食物,这意味着中国融入全球多元文化的现状。

2. 总结性评估

总结性评估采取测试和口试的方式来检测学生对于课程目标的达成。

例(一)我们根据布鲁姆目标分类方法来检测学生在知识、认识和深度思考领域的目标是否达成。

Evaluation	评价
Synthesis	综合
Analysis	分析
Application	应用
Comprehension	领会
Knowledge	知识

课程目标与实施　005

例（二）引入批判思维测试来检测学生深度思考的能力。

1. What are the ways of knowing? (4 points)

2. What are the advantages and disadvantages of sense perception as a way of knowing? (4 points)

3. What are the features of memory? Please name at least 4 and explain one of them. (6 points)

例（三）通过古诗词分析测试学生的分析能力。

Part Three (10 points)

Read the poem written by Du Fu, and analyze how this poem is related to the traditional Chinese philosophy. (at least 100 words)

The poem was written by Du Fu when he was 56 years old. At that time, he was ill and alone. When the poet reached the top of the mountain and saw the view of autumn, he composed the poem.

登高

杜甫

风急天高猿啸哀，渚清沙白鸟飞回。
无边落木萧萧下，不尽长江滚滚来。
万里悲秋常作客，百年多病独登台。
艰难苦恨繁霜鬓，潦倒新停浊酒杯。

View From a Height

The winds cut, clouds are high,
apes wail their sorrows.
The air is fresh, sand white,
birds fly in circles.
On all sides fallen leaves
go rustling, rusting.
While ceaseless river waves
come rippling, rippling.
Autumn's each faded mile
seems like my journey.
To mount, alone and ill,
to this balcony.

Life's failures and regrets
frosting my temples.
And wretched that I've had
to give up drinking.

探索世界篇

课案一

中西茶文化对比

课程设计教师：

王靖雯

英语语言文学硕士

VCE EAL 执教资格认证

IB English B 执教资格认证

从事托福、雅思、SAT 教学多年，具有丰富的教学经验，善于发现学生个体问题并制订相应的教学计划，进行有针对性的教学。对国内课程体系和国际课程的融合有一定的思考和研究。

内容：

一、课程设置背景

二、课程内容

三、课程目的和意义

四、课程核心思想

五、授课过程

一、课程设置背景

我国 2010 年颁布的《国家中长期教育改革和发展规划纲要（2010—2020年）》、2011 年颁布的《义务教育课程标准（2011 年版）》等重要文件中，都提出了"加强国际理解教育，推动跨文化交流，增进学生对不同国家、不同文化的认识和理解"等要求。

然而中国教育国际化仍然处于探索性阶段。目前，中国各地开展的国际化课程尚缺乏一个完整的教学体系和模式，尤其是基础教育国际化进程中往往采用国际理解类课程和传统文化国学课程孤立开设的形式，忽略了教育国际化的"双向交流"需求。同时，因为缺乏一些资源，国际理解类课程也暂时未能落地生根。

国际理解课程应拥有立足本土文化的课程载体，让学生从认识和思考身边事物开始，逐步走出自己所熟悉的世界，用更广阔的眼光认识世界。我们的教研团队开发了以中国茶文化为载体，集历史、人文、视觉艺术、经济学、生物、数学于一体的国际理解和国际融合课程。学生通过学习与茶叶相关的历史、文化、视觉艺术、经济学、生物、数学等内容进行前期相关知识的储备，最终的成果是以茶叶博览会的形式，围绕"茶与茶文化""茶与茶具""茶叶销售"等方面，将在6节课中所学到的内容通过海报、陈述等方式进行展示。

《成都市中长期教育改革和发展规划纲要（2010—2020年)》和《成都市教育国际化发展专项规划（2013—2020年)》指出，要深化教育对外交流与合作，拓展广大中小学生的国际视野，增强国际意识，提升国际素养，加强中小学国际理解教育。国际化教育强调的是国际视野，但其前提却是民族情怀。古为今用，洋为中用，只有尊重和认同本民族文化，才能尊重和理解不同民族、地域、国家的文化。因此，我们的主题选题是"川茶"。四川具有悠久的茶叶文化，渗透在百姓生活之中，同学们相对熟悉，比较容易将自己的观察或者其他方面的生活经验代入对知识的理解中，达到双向促进的作用。

二、课程内容

1. 中国部分

内容包括中国茶的起源和分类、川茶与茶马古道的历史、中国茶如何通过茶马古道传到欧洲各地。

通过对课程内容的介绍，让学生了解中国茶的起源和茶马古道的历史，引导学生了解中国茶如何对世界产生影响。

2. 国际部分

内容包括下午茶的起源和传统、品下午茶及其礼仪。

通过对课程内容的介绍，引导学生对比思考中国茶文化和英国茶文化之间的相似点和不同点，引导学生简单描述中国茶文化的特点并启发学生思考如何尊重他人文化，理解文化差异。

三、课程目的和意义

跨学科主题：历史＋中西方文化差异

通过介绍中国茶的起源、茶马古道的历史以及英式下午茶的喝法，让学生了解茶文化如何从中国传到世界各个国家，并思考茶在人们生活中的影响；让学生认识日常生活中中西方文化的特点以及中西方文化的差异；激发学生学习英语的兴趣，培养学生的跨文化意识。

四、课程核心思想

这样的教学方式有助于同学们拓宽国际视野，对不同的文化习俗具有包容度并懂得尊重他人。

教学目标：

(1) 中国部分。

学生能够独立讲述中国茶的起源和分类。

学生能够在地图上大致画出茶马古道的走向。

学生能够了解茶叶在中国历史上的重要作用。

(2) 国际部分。

学生能够大致描述下午茶的起源。

学生能够准确说出茶具和茶点的名字。

学生能够说出中国茶和英式下午茶的1～3个相似点或不同点。

通过对不同茶文化进行对比分析，训练学生的逻辑表达能力和批判性思维。

五、授课过程

（一）中国部分

1. 课程引入

由音乐视频《刘三姐》引入中国茶叶的主题。

2. 新课内容

从"茶之义""茶之源""茶之境""茶之路"四个方面为同学们介绍中国茶叶的知识。

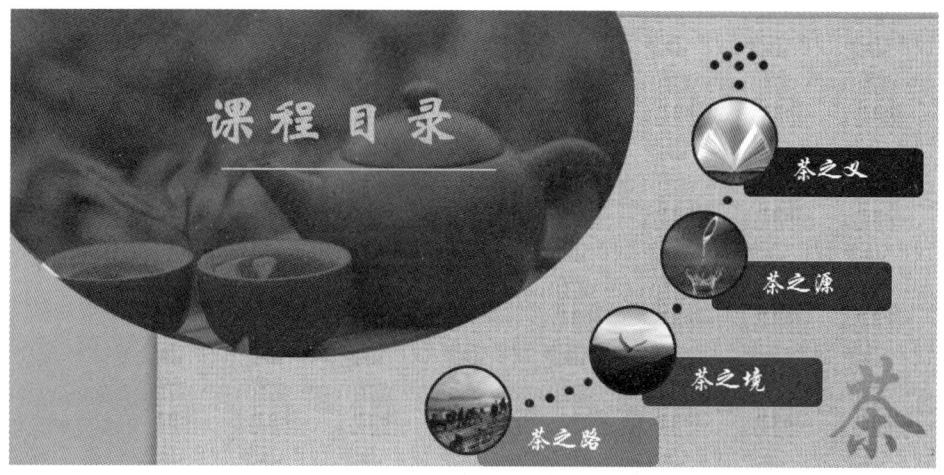

一段神农尝百草的故事让同学们在神话故事中开启对茶叶起源的思考，紧接着陆羽的《茶经》和西南的地方性著作《华阳国志》向同学们展现了茶叶起源于南方的诸多猜想。在"茶之境"中，教师为同学们展示了四川特有的茶文化，包括四川茶馆、成都盖碗茶等。盖碗虽然是一种不起眼的茶具，但是它蕴含了中国人最朴素的哲学思想——天时、地利、人和。同时，教师也可以引导同学对比中式和西式茶具的不同。在"茶之路"中，同学们积极思考世界上哪些国家的人们爱喝茶且有着悠久的茶叶历史文化，以此加强对世界的认知。紧接着同学们可以学习四川的茶叶如何通过茶马古道走出中国，走向世界，加强了中国与世界的联系。

（二）国际部分

喝下午茶，在当今社会，不仅是成年人喜爱的放松方式，还受到越来越多青少年的喜爱。除了有美味的茶点，更重要的是它已逐渐成为一种社交休闲的重要途径。但同学们对下午茶的了解比较笼统，尤其是在中国这样一个以茶文化而著名的国家，同学们不仅对中国茶文化的历史知之甚少，而且对世界范围内茶文化的发展也没有系统的学习。作为全球化发展趋势下的新一代，这些未来的世界公民们不仅需要了解本国茶文化，还需要对西方茶文化的发展和礼仪建立起基本的认知，因此，英式下午茶的课程应运而生。

1. 英式下午茶的起源

当安娜公爵夫人的图片出现在大屏幕上时，同学们对这个重要人物的故事或许还并不了解。通过讲解，同学们知道了现在非常流行的下午茶起源于英国一位名叫安娜的公爵夫人。从她的故事里，大家认识了英式下午茶的历史起源。

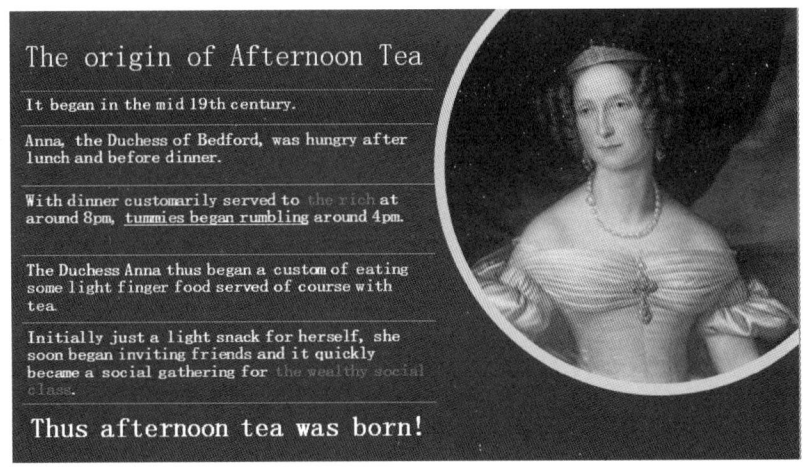

2. 下午茶的种类

当讲到英式下午茶的分类时，同学们对四种不同的下午茶名称展开议论。对于"High Tea""Low Tea""Cream Tea""Royal Tea"，大家单从字面上理解猜测，都觉得"Royal Tea"是最高级的，因为其字面意思就是"皇家茶"，而对于"Low Tea"，大家都一致觉得它应该比较低档，而另外一种"High Tea"，一定是"高大上"的下午茶。当教师一一介绍这四种不同的英式下午茶的名称来源和背后的故事，大家才发现，"Low Tea"这个名称比较有误导性,没想到它居然是英国贵族最爱的主流下午茶模式,叫这个名字仅仅是因为他们饮茶的桌子是低矮的茶几。与此相反的是,"High Tea"并不是我们想象中的"高大上"的下午茶,而是英国工人阶层喜爱的下午茶类型,因为工人们都是在高高的工作台旁边直接站着喝下午茶,并且这个下午茶最重要的目的不是放松或社交,而是为了填饱肚子继续下午的劳作,所以这种下午茶里的茶点与其他三种下午茶截然不同,主要是以面包、肉类为主。大家觉得最高级的"Royal Tea"也并不是只有皇室才能享用的下午茶,它与其他下午茶唯一的区别就是,它是可以喝香槟而不喝茶的下午茶。听到这些,同学们都开始感叹,了解文字背后的历史文化才是最重要的,这样深入的学习不仅可以更多地了解西方茶文化,还可以避免犯一些因为无知造成的尴尬错误。

Is royal tea really for the royals?

- Of course not. Royal tea does not refer to tea for the royals. Instead, it's another type of afternoon tea but with Champagne!

3. 下午茶器皿及礼仪

在了解了下午茶的基本分类及含义后,我们通过图片和实物展示相结合的方式,给同学们介绍了传统英式下午茶的主要茶具器皿,让大家明白这些茶具的英文表达以及正确的使用方法。在下午茶礼仪环节,通过一个个小问题,让同学们根据自己的理解自由表达、各抒己见,在讨论和讲解中理清每一个问题,并且形成对下午茶基本礼仪的认知。

1. The utensil and food (choosing & matching)

> A. 茶具　B. 茶匙　C. 茶托　D. 茶壶　E. 茶杯　F. 蛋糕架
>
> G. 餐巾纸　H. 司康饼　I. 果酱　J. 奶油　K. 三明治　L. 下午茶

Tea pot _____ Saucer _____

Cake stand _____ Tea cup _____

Napkin _____ Tea spoon _____

Utensil _____ sandwich _____

Jam _____ scone _____

Cream _____ low tea _____

2. The Afternoon Tea Etiquette (Q&A)

Q1: What should people wear when they have afternoon tea?
_____

Q2: How to use napkin when having afternoon tea?
_____

Q3: Do you know how to stir your tea correctly?
_____

Q4: How to hold your tea cup properly?
_____

Q5: What should eat first from the three-tiered cake stand?
_____

Q6: Can you write down some food on the cake stand?
_____

Q7: Can you take big bites when eating? Why or Why not?
_____

课堂活动中的题单

Activity: Interview

- Pair Work
- The interviewer:
- Ask questions about afternoon tea. (the origin, the utensil, the food, the etiquette)
- The interviewee:
- Answer the questions based on what we learn about afternoon tea.

课堂活动一

4. 学生成果展示

在充分了解四种不同的英式下午茶的内涵和礼仪后，同学们组队商讨开办自己的下午茶小店，并且精心设计了以茶为主题的各种茶产品海报，大力宣传自己的下午茶小店和茶产品。一张张富有创意的海报，让大家对下午茶有了更深刻的认识和理解。

探索世界篇 *017*

课堂活动二

学生现场展示小组作品

通过这样的学习,同学们对西方茶文化有了更深入的了解。中国作为产茶大国,茶文化历史悠久。学生不仅要了解本国茶文化,更要放眼全球,对中西茶文化有全面的了解和认知,在多方位学习发展中培养全球视野,避免因文化差异引起的冲突和误解,成为具有国际视野的全面发展的世界公民。

课案二

从经济学角度分析茶馆的收益与成本

课程设计教师：

周城晨

硕士研究生，毕业于英国爱丁堡大学经济学专业

7年经济学教学经验

AP 经济学执教资质认证

内容：

一、课程背景

二、驱动问题

三、课程推进

四、活动任务

五、活动总结

六、活动升华

一、课程背景

国家经济的增长与发展离不开一群拥有探索和创新精神的企业家。在本课茶文化的项目式学习中，经济学科将以成都茶馆文化作为切入点，让学生理解成立一家公司时所面临的机遇与挑战，理解企业家经营的目标之一是实现利润最大化。通过小组讨论、理论讲解以及学生活动，教师渐进式地启发学生思考企业面临的决策，鼓励学生像企业家一样进行决策分析，从而实现企业的目

标,最后进行总结和反思。

二、驱动问题

在我们的茶馆主题下,学生首先需要探讨以及解决的问题是:自主创业开一家茶馆前,创业者需要思考哪些问题?

围绕开茶馆这一问题,学生们将进行头脑风暴,他们思考的问题包括:
(1)经营茶馆的目的是什么?
(2)茶馆卖什么产品?
(3)茶馆卖多少产品?
(4)茶馆的产量受哪些因素影响?
(5)茶馆如何组织生产?
(6)茶馆生产面临的成本有哪些?

三、课程推进

经济学是研究稀缺资源如何进行合理配置的一门学科,它要解决的三大问题包括:生产什么?生产多少?如何生产?就宏观层面而言,这是社会要解决的资源配置。就微观层面而言,这是每个企业要进行的决策。本堂课程从微观层面出发,研究企业的决策问题,思考企业家的选择。

学生分小组讨论自己新开的茶馆卖的产品、计划的产量以及如何组织生产。讨论小组继续思考"经营茶馆的目的是什么?"大部分学生会谈到以赚钱或者实现利润最大化为目标。从经济学角度分析,企业的目标之一是实现利润最大化。但教师可以借此引导学生拓展思维,思考企业经营的其他目标,如实现社会责任等非营利性目标。由非营利性目标又可以引导学生进一步思考企业家的情怀,尤其是当企业有足够的市场影响力后,该如何更好地利用企业去实现社会价值。

接着,教师可以引入经济概念,如"利润""固定成本""可变成本""利润=收益-成本"等,并且举例说明经营茶馆面临的固定成本、可变成本有哪些,介绍固定成本、可变成本如何在短期或者长期中影响企业的决策。

确定"实现利润最大化"是企业经营的目标之一后,学生继续讨论"如何增加自己新建茶馆的利润"。学生讨论时会提到增加收益和减少成本两种方式。教师继续引导学生深入思考:增加收益和减少成本的方式包括哪些?

四、活动任务

利用小棒和棉花糖搭建一座茶馆,茶馆盖得越高,容纳的客人越多,收益就越大,但同时花费的成本也越高。通过分小组进行游戏,同学们像企业家一样进行决策,目标是实现新建茶馆的利润最大化。

活动按以下步骤进行:

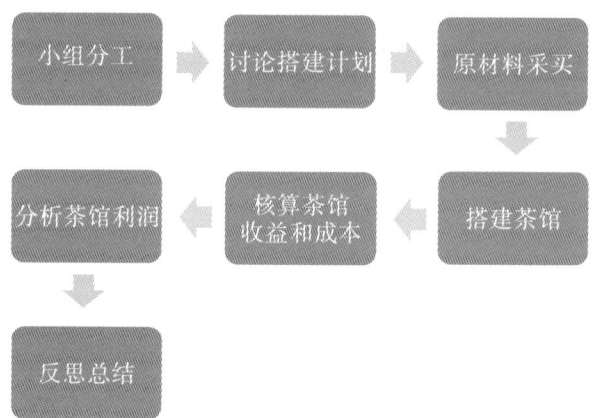

小组分工（确定每位同学的工作）

职务	职责	负责人（填上相关同学姓名）
策划员（Planner，1人）	提出建设方案	
采购员（Purchaser，1人）	保管发票，购买原材料	
建筑师（Builder，1人）	监管茶馆建设	
工人（Worker，2人）	搭建茶馆	
经理（Manager，1人）	协调其他职员，确保按时完工	

收益（Profit）
• 10厘米以下的茶馆，每厘米收益400元
• 10厘米以上的茶馆，超出10厘米的部分，每厘米收益800元（如某茶馆高12厘米，那么其总收益为 400×10+800×2=5600元）
• 最佳设计茶馆，格外获得2000元奖励
• 最牢固茶馆（能支撑1张白纸超过5秒钟的），额外获得3000元奖励

固定成本	
房租（Rent）	500元
保险（Insurance）	100元
固定成本总数	

可变成本	
小棒（Stick）	100元/根
棉花糖（Marshmallow）	50元/个
未用的材料	50元/个
损坏的材料	200元/个
被吃了的棉花糖	100元/个

采购发票（Purchasing Invoice）

物品	数量	单价	总价
（例）小棒	8	100元	800元
加上未使用的材料，每个50元			
加上损坏的材料，每个200元			
加上被吃掉的棉花糖，每个100元			
可变成本总数			

续表

物品	数量	单价	总价
固定成本总数			600元
总成本（可变成本＋固定成本）			

总收益	
茶馆的总高度为：　　厘米　　　　超过10厘米的高度为：　　厘米	
低于10厘米部分的收益，每厘米400元	
高于10厘米部分的收益，每厘米800元	
最佳设计茶馆，额外奖励2000元	
最牢固茶馆，额外奖励3000元	
总收益	

五、活动总结

确定各小组的收益、成本和利润。各小组总结茶馆搭建过程中遇到的困难、影响其利润高低的因素以及计划如何改进提高利润。学生通过活动会发现成本收益分析的理论与实际应用的差别。

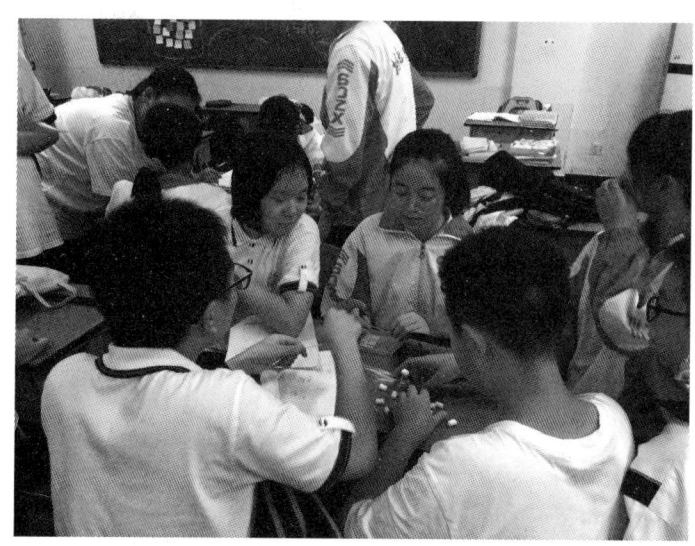

六、课程升华

学生在实际操作搭建茶馆时都会面临很多无法预料的事宜,包括如何将小棒和棉花糖进行组合搭建茶馆、购买的原材料不足或过多等问题,因此导致最终实际获得的利润与计划的利润存在较大的差异。

教师可以启发学生思考理论与实际操作出现差异的原因,作为企业家成立一家企业时可能面临的困难,以及此活动对个人选择的指导意义。

课案三

韩国人口危机

课程设计教师：

Calvin McDonald was born in Banbury, Oxfordshire, England in 1988. At the age of eight, he traveled across the sea to America where he spent the rest of his childhood and eventually attended university at The University of Oklahoma. In 2012, he received a Bachelor of Arts in history with an emphasis on world history and a minor in Chinese language. Calvin has lived in Chengdu, China for the past seven years teaching a range of courses at the high school level, such as Introduction to American Culture, IELTS Speaking, English for Academic Purposes, and most notably IB English B. In his spare time, Calvin enjoys increasing his Chinese language proficiency, chowing down on chuan chuan（串串）, and visiting obscure art galleries in different corners of Chengdu.

内容：

1. Introduction
2. Objectives
3. Activity 1: How to Plot a Pyramid Graph
4. Activity 2: What is Causing Low Birth Rates
5. Activity 3: Poster Presentation
6. Activity 4: Grammar Exploration

1. Introduction

Issues of population, particularly overpopulation, have been of public interest since the time of Thomas Robert Malthus, the 19th-century English political economist who wrote the 1798 treatise, *An Essay on the Principle of Population*. Some of his fears of overpopulation still resonate with many today who remember the 20th-century, or at least the latter part of the 20th century, as a time when the idea was put forth that the overconsumption and use of resources, such as water, forests, and wildlife, would inevitably bring about the downfall of developed societies and the rest of the world in short order. In order to counteract the consequences of this overconsumption stemming from overpopulation, government initiatives across the world were taken to reserve resources and decrease population totals. Some of the most well-known initiatives have been the emphasis on educating women with the belief that an educated woman would have fewer children and policies focused on restricting the number of children a woman could bear, as seen in China's One-Child Policy. While such initiatives certainly helped to remedy issues brought about by industrialization and overpopulation, one issue that hadn't been given much consideration was what effect lower birth rates would have on nation-states as they made the transition from developed nations to post-industrialized nations.

In this unit, I felt discussing the consequences and possible solutions of aging populations and lower birth rates with students would help students understand how economic progress, government policies, and culture are intricately connected, and hopefully in the process encourage the students to take an active role in promoting policies and ideas that will not only help those countries that have already reached their post-industrialized phase navigate demographic issues but also help those countries that have yet to reach it become better prepared.

2. Objectives

By the end of this unit, the students shall have mastered the following objectives:

• Learn to create and analyze a pyramid graph.
• Understand the development of industrialization and how it relates to demographics.
• Understand the consequences of an aging and declining population on society.
• Successfully analyze the policies of government and their effectiveness as well as create your own policy suggestions.
• Understand how the experiences of nations like South Korea might have important implications for your own country and countries around the world.
• Understand and practice "If Conditionals".

Throughout this unit, students will analyze pyramid charts to discover how population distribution changes as societies transition from non-industrialized societies to post-industrialized societies. Along the way, they will learn how to read population data and plot it on a chart according to age, sex, and percentage of the total population. This unit will mainly focus on the demographics of South Korea, and, we will be looking at what role South Korea's culture, as compared to other societies, such as American culture, has played in either helping South Korea's demographic issues or further deteriorating them. Activities will be assigned to the students that encourage them to use critical thinking skills as well as research skills to discover what issues have been brought about by South Korea's declining and aging population. In addition, students will analyze the initiatives South Korea's government has proposed to combat the issue and whether or not these solutions have been effective as well as whether or not the issue can truly be resolved by government or if a different approach is needed. Finally, we will round the unit out by understanding where our own country of origin stands in the evolution of industrialization and what lessons countries that have yet to industrialize, such as countries in Africa, can learn in order to avoid facing demographic issues in the future.

3. Activity 1: How to Plot a Pyramid Graph

In the first activity, How to Plot a Pyramid Graph, students will use South Korea's demographic data from the years 1958, 2018, and 2045 to plot pyramid charts of South Korea's population. Each student will receive one handout of image A and be given 10 minutes to complete all three charts. For many students, the procedure needed to fill out each graph will be very apparent, but in order to differentiate the lesson, it is recommended that the instructor fills out the year 1958 prior to teaching the activity and then uses the completed chart to help students understand how each age band is plotted and recognize what the completed chart will look like. Upon completion of each graph, students can work in groups or alone to answer some extension questions about the finished graphs.

Year	Sex	0-4	5-9	10-14	15-19	20-24	25-29	30-34	35-39	40-44	45-49	50-54	55-59	60-64	65-69	70-74	75-79	80-84	85-89	90-94	95-99	100+
1958	Male	9.0%	7.0%	5.9%	5.2%	4.5%	3.2%	2.9%	2.8%	2.3%	2.1%	1.7%	1.2%	1.0%	0.7%	0.4%	0.2%	0.1%	0.0%	0.0%	0.0%	0.0%
1958	Female	8.6%	6.4%	5.4%	4.8%	4.4%	3.8%	3.2%	2.8%	2.3%	2.1%	1.6%	1.3%	1.2%	0.9%	0.6%	0.3%	0.1%	0.0%	0.0%	0.0%	0.0%
2018	Male	2.1%	2.3%	2.3%	2.8%	3.5%	3.6%	3.5%	3.9%	4.1%	4.3%	4.2%	4.0%	3.3%	2.2%	1.7%	1.2%	0.7%	0.3%	0.1%	0.0%	0.0%
2018	Female	2.0%	2.2%	2.2%	2.6%	3.1%	3.1%	3.2%	3.7%	3.9%	4.2%	4.2%	4.0%	3.4%	2.4%	2.0%	1.7%	1.2%	0.6%	0.2%	0.1%	0.0%
2045	Male	1.6%	1.7%	1.8%	1.8%	1.9%	2.1%	2.5%	2.5%	2.8%	3.5%	3.8%	3.5%	3.8%	3.8%	3.9%	3.4%	2.7%	1.7%	0.6%	0.1%	0.0%
2045	Female	1.5%	1.6%	1.7%	1.7%	1.8%	2.0%	2.3%	2.3%	2.5%	3.2%	3.3%	3.2%	3.7%	3.8%	4.1%	4.0%	3.5%	2.6%	1.2%	0.4%	0.1%

Questions:

(1) How did the number of young people (age 0－24) change from the years 1958 to 2045? What might explain this change?

(2) Looking at men and women, how did the ratio of men and women change from age 0 to age 100＋? What might explain this?

(3) How can understanding the demographics of a country be useful?

Activity: Extension

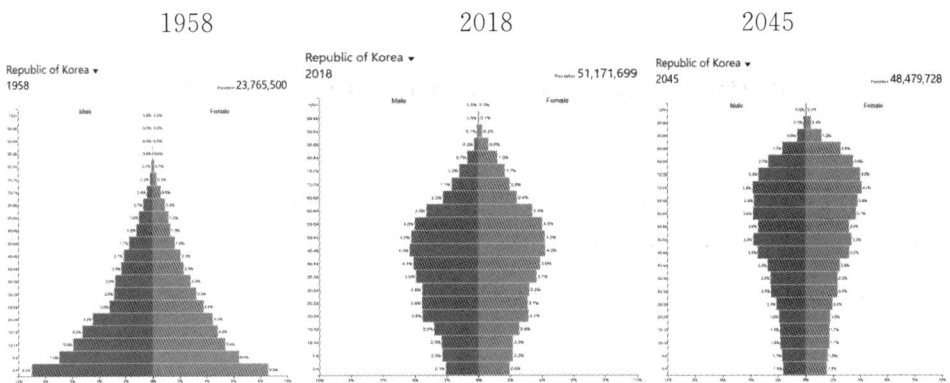

In the extension part of our first activity, students and teachers participate in class discussion. The class discusses in what ways these three graphs are different. The class should conclude that the earliest graph (1958) shows the highest percentage of young individuals, the 2018 graph shows the highest percentage of middle-aged individuals, and the last graph (2048) shows the highest percentage of elderly individuals. After this has been determined, students are asked to break into groups and match each graph to one of three choices: pre-industrial, industrialized, or post-industrialized. Once the students have split each pyramid graph up based on the three given choices, the students must then explain their reasons for why they split them up the way they did. Finally, the teacher should explain why these three graphs have different populations proportions by explaining that pre-industrialized countries usually rely heavily on agriculture and infant mortality is quite high. This situation makes having many children a necessity, which ultimately leads to a large young population, as can be seen in the 1958 graph. As nations industrialize, migration to cities takes place, and in the cities, infant mortality decreases and less children are needed because farm work does not exist. This leads to lower birth rates in industrialized nations. However, the high birth rate of years prior does supply the industrialized economy with a large middle-aged working class. As nations enter their post-industrialized phase, birth rates continue to remain flat and, in some cases, turn negative, and the large working class of the industrial phase enter their senior years, which is why the 2048 graph shows elderly individuals increasing while new births remain relatively unchanged.

4. Activity 2: What is Causing Low Birth Rates

In this activity, students learn what is causing the decrease in birth rates in South Korea by reading the article, "South Korea Sees More Deaths Than Births." Afterwards, students answer questions to gauge their comprehension.

South Korea Sees More Deaths Than Births for 1st Time

The number of deaths in South Korea exceeded the number of babies born there last year for the first time in the country's history, prompting calls for stronger policies and incentives to revamp demographic growth and sustain the economy.

Births in 2020 were down 10.65% compared to the previous year at 275,815, while deaths were up 3.1% to 307,764, according to the South Korean Ministry of the Interior and Safety's census. South Korea's population currently stands at 51,839,408.

"This drop in population is an extremely dire situation," Jung Chounsook, a women's rights activist and member of South Korea's National Assembly, told ABC News.

South Korea has the lowest fertility rate of any nation in the world, at 0.84, meaning less than one child is born to a mother. The global average is around 2.4 children, according to the United Nations Population Fund.

"In South Korean society, marriages and births cost a considerable lump sum of money. So financial burdens are a big factor," Cho Youngtae, a demography professor at Seoul National University in South Korea's capital, told ABC News. "The economic situation has worsened due to the pandemic, the future is therefore even more uncertain, which means less weddings."

Marriages registered nationwide last year fell 9% compared to the year before, according to Statistics Korea data, indicating birth rates this year will most likely fall steeper than 2020.

Analysts like Eun Ki-Soo, head of the Population Association of Korea, said the reasons why South Korean society is recording such dismal birth rates are complex but that, fundamentally, it comes down to the financial uncertainties that young South Koreans face for the future.

"Economic growth has staggered, there are less jobs, poverty has risen, and the housing shortages. All these have generally affected the population to shrink in the past decades," he told ABC News.

In reality, 70.9% of young men over the age of 19 in South Korea rely on their parents to provide housing, according to a 2020 survey conducted by online recruiting company SaraminHR. Only 29.9% of newlyweds last year were able to afford housing during the first year into marriage, with many supported by their parents, according to Statistics Korea data. Real estate prices have soared to record highs, and it's estimated to take more than 15 years to buy an average priced house, even if one saves his or her entire income, according to the Korea Real Estate Board's projection last year.

"The fact that marriage and childbirth lead to disadvantage in promotion or personnel transfers at work holds me back from forming a family," said Kim Dongkyu, a plastic surgeon in his early 30s who is firm with his choice to stay single.

Even if a couple weds, planning a family is a far-fetched dream in modern South Korea where people are known to spend unsparingly on children's education. In 2019, over $19 billion was spent on private education in addition to regular school classes, according to the South Korean Ministry of Education. Three out of four students in elementary, middle, and high schools received some kind of extracurricular private education. On average, parents spent approximately $300 on a child's private after-school tutoring each month.

In an effort to combat the falling marriage and birth rates, the South Korean government has implemented a series of policies and initiatives, including cash incentives. Starting in 2022, every pregnant woman will receive 1 million won ($919.5), then 2 million won ($1,839.1) upon birth. And if both parents opt for childcare leave within the first year of birth, each parent will receive 3 million won ($2,758.6) for three months. Benefits expand for multi-child families, with subsidies offered for college education.

But Eunjin Shin, a 33-year-old bank teller in Seoul, told ABC News that "no one I know makes the decision to have kids based on government policies." She gave birth to her second child last year.

"My district gave me $275 for my second child, although nothing for my firstborn," Shin said. "Monthly subsidies barely cover the cost of diapers, and we pay a babysitter extra from a completely separate pocket."

For a young, working mother of two like Kim Hojeong, these cash bonuses barely cover what she pays her babysitter—about $2,000 a month. "Government grant helps when purchasing hundreds of baby products, but it will never solve the low birth rate," Hojeong told ABC News. "What we want is an environment with flexible working hours and affordable public childcare that you can trust."

Source: *www.abcnews.go.com*

Author: Joohee Cho

Date: Jan. 5th 2021

Comprehension Questions:

(1) According to the article, what country has the lowest birth rate in the world? What is the average?

(2) What is the biggest factor affecting the birth rate in South Korea?

(3) What percentage of men over the age of 19 in South Korea depend on their parents for housing?

(4) The article estimates that it would take the average South Korean how many years to buy a house?

(5) Why does Kim Dongkyu prefer to stay single?

(6) What has the South Korean government done to help incentivize births?

(7) Do Eunjin Shin and Kim Hojeong feel the government's efforts are impactful?

(8) What does Kim Hojeong suggest a better approach might be?

Activity: Debate

Government Intervention or Increased Immigration?

Two of the methods that have been put forth to help remedy the issues of low birth rates are:

(1) Incentivizing couples to have more than one child through government incentives such as subsidies.

(2) Increasing immigration into countries that need a younger demographic.

Task:

Split the class into two groups. One group should research government programs used to increase childbirths and the other group should research increased immigration. Once each group has finished researching, they can debate which solution they believe is most appropriate.

5. Activity 3: Poster Presentation

For a population to continue growing and meeting the demands of not only a country's workforce but also the needs of its elderly population, a woman on average must have 2.1 children. In the case of South Korea, the decline in the population has been created through economic as well as societal pressures but in some instances, a decline in population numbers can be attributed to an artificially created decline, as is the case with China.

In 1979, China enacted its One-Child Policy. Under the policy, couples were allowed to have at most one child. The policy was created to control the growth of China's population which totaled well above 1 billion citizens. China's citizens acclimated to the new policy well and it was widely regarded as a success but with one downside being that it forced China's birth rate below the 2.1 childbirths per woman threshold.

In 2016, the One-Child Policy was officially ended and couples were allowed to have two children. The new policy should help China to navigate the demographic issues that other developed nations around the world have faced, but convincing China's citizens to have more children has been easier said than done.

Source: National Geographic

Activity:

In this activity, the student's task is to create a poster that will encourage the citizens of China to have more children. Afterwards, they must present the poster in front of the class.

Requirements:

• Group work

• One poster per group

• Presentation must be at least 5 minutes long

6. Activity 4: Grammar Exploration

If conditionals, which are sometimes called "if clauses", are used to describe the results of things that have happened in the present or the future or might have occurred in the past. There are four types of conditionals known as the zero conditional, first conditional, second conditional, and third conditionals.

Zero Conditional: Describes general truths and habits.

If + present simple, present simple.

Example: If you drop an apple, it falls.

First Conditional: Describes things that will happen in the future if conditions are met.

If + present simple, will + present simple.

Example: If you give me money, I will buy a gift.

Second Conditional: Describes things unlikely to happen in the future.

If + past simple, would + infinitive.

Example: If I had a car, I would drive to Las Vegas.

Third Conditional: Describes things that did not happen in the past and the results if they had happened.

If + past perfect, would + have + past participle.

Example: If I had ran harder, I would have won the race.

Activity: Grammar Practice

Fill in the blank with the correct response based on the type of conditional.

1. (Conditional 2) If I _____ (win) a cat, I _____ (give) it to my mother.

2. (Conditional 0) If you _____ (drop) an apple from a tower, it _____ (fall).

3. (Conditional 3) If she _____ (go) to my birthday party, she _____ (have) a good time.

4. (Conditional 1) If you _____ (find) my dog, I _____ (give) you a reward.

5. (Conditional 2) If my brother _____ (be) rich, he _____ (have) a huge house.

课案四

中西节日对比研究

课程设计教师：
游佳
ETS 托福讲师
12 年英语教学经验
TEDx 英语演讲活动评委及主持人
剑桥 KET/PET 考试口语考官
内容：
一、课程背景
二、课程理念
三、课程目标
四、课程内容
五、课程反思

一、课程背景

随着人类社会的不断进步，信息革命的不断深入，地球已经成为"地球村"，每个孩子都有了一个新的称号——"全球公民"。任何交流的实现已经不再受到距离的阻碍，在不可逆转的国际化形势下，如何面对不确定的未来，如何创新思考，走向世界，为未来的国际事务做出贡献是每一个孩子需要直面的问题。教育要面向未来，在这样的思考之下，国际理解课程应运而生，根据最新的全球胜任力模型，国际理解课程希望能够培养出脚踏中国根基、拥有全球视野的未来公民,他们既要掌握作为硬能力的人文科技素养与外语能力,也要身兼作为软实力的国际人才核心素养,具备处理国际事务的知识和能力,拥有人类命运共同体的意识,成为适应国际化形势的人才。

树德中学国际理解课程的目标是彰显本国文化自信,让学生在了解本国文化和他国文化的基础之上进行平等的文化对话和交流,让学生们拥有大国气场;以国际平台为视觉的立足点来观察和理解事物,发展认知能力,扩大眼界和心胸,克服思想的狭隘、偏见,以人类命运共同体的认知为前提,以知识为基础,理解各种现象背后的文化差异;能够了解世界事务处理的相关机构,世界事务发展的规律以及规则,培养能够站在国际理解的角度发出中国声音的高质量人才。

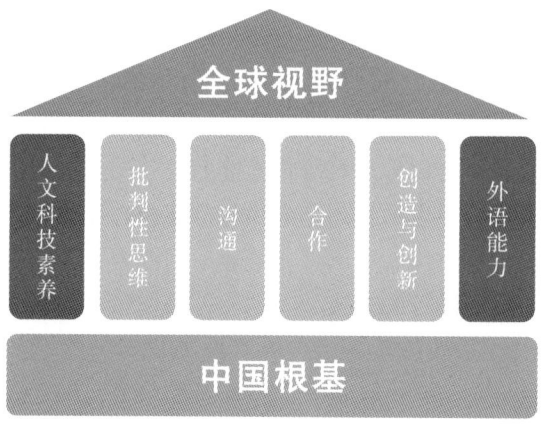

二、课程理念

节日是一个国家文化的集中表现,节日的差异能够极大地反映其背后文化的差异。理解中国和西方节日的特点并知道其背后的文化原因有助于提高学生对文化差异的感知,撬动元认知能力,通过文化的碰撞提高反思自身文化的能力,提高学生从多个角度理解和看待问题的能力,以及站在不同的文化角度换位思考的能力,从而达到国际理解的目的。

课程难度:根据布鲁姆分类法(Bloom's Taxonomy)认知的几个阶段来设计课程难度。

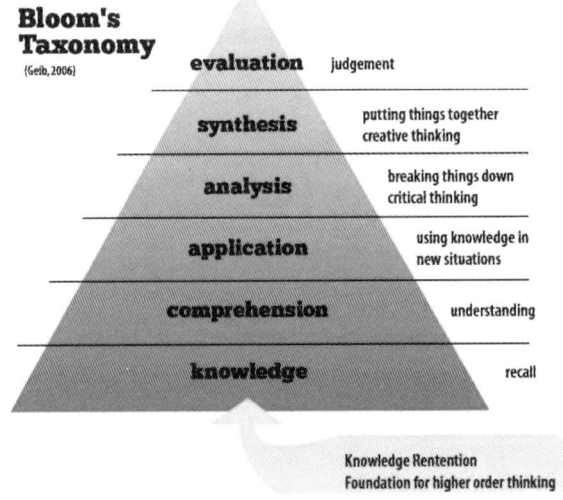

首先让学生了解中国春节的文化习俗和西方圣诞节的文化习俗,知道如何用英文描述这些文化节日,通过对比不同的文化现象探讨两种节日背后的文化原因,理解不同文化风格的存在;再通过提取相同的元素了解节日对于各国人民的意义,理解节日在文化传承和情感连接上的共同意义,促进对不同文化的尊重和认同。为了培养学生的批判思维和分析能力,让学生分析节日带来的利与弊和节日在商业领域应用的案例。在培养运用能力方面,可以引导学生思考让春节在年轻人中更加流行的方式。

三、课程目标

语言目标：
（1）学会与春节和圣诞节相关的常用英文表达。
（2）能够用英语介绍春节和圣诞节的特点。
（3）能够运用对比表达的句型说明差异。

文化目标：
（1）了解中国春节的习俗和西方圣诞节的习俗。
（2）比较两个节日的差异和共同之处。
（3）分析差异背后的文化原因。

思维目标：
（1）分析节日存在的意义。
（2）分析节日给我们带来的好处和坏处。
（3）如何让我们的节日传承下去？

情感目标：
促进文化的认同和尊重。

课堂活动：
（1）分类 Classification（brief warm-up）
（2）比较 Comparison（half-guided practice）
（3）体验式课堂 Experience in Class（剪窗花和画圣诞贺卡）
（4）介绍一个新节日（墨西哥 piñata）
（5）送祝福活动 Expressing Gratitude

四、课程内容

1. Lead in

Give students two symbols of Spring Festival and Christmas.

Warm-up questions:

What do the two pictures represent?

What do we usually do during Spring Festival?

Give more key words about Spring Festival.

What do people do during Christmas?

Give more key words about Christmas.

2. Class Activities

Classify the events into Spring Festival or Christmas:

paper cutting   fireworks and firecrackers   dumplings   Santa Claus
television gala   turkey   fish   couplets   family reunion
lucky money   stockings   sending wishes

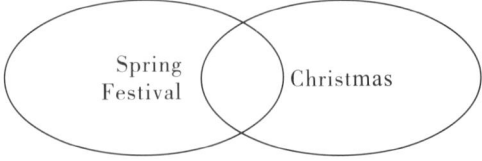

3. Class Content

(1) 请同学们阅读一篇英语文章"Chinese Spring Festival VS Christmas"并填写表格,从不同的方面对文章内容进行分类,填好之后的表格呈现如下。

Read an article and fill in the table:

Aspects	Spring Festival	Christmas
Time and duration	The first day of the Chinese Lunar Calendar; about two weeks	December 25; about two weeks
Food	Fish and dumplings (Jiaozi); meal time: in the evening of Chinese New Year's Eve	Turkey, nuts, sweets, and cakes; meal time: at lunchtime of Christmas Day
Present	Hong Bao (lucky money in red envelop) given by seniors and new clothes	Toys for kids given by Santa Claus; adults exchange fruit baskets, sweets, alcohol, tea and other items; hang stockings by the fireplace, hoping Santa will fill them with gifts
Legends	Monster Nian	Tales of the historical Saint Nicholas (Santa Claus) and the mythical embodiment of Christmas (father Christmas) merge into one benevolent present-giver
Sound	Loud Firecrackers and fireworks	Aesthetically pleasing fireworks
Colors and decorations	Red and gold; couplets with good wishes, paper cutting, images in relation to the Chinese zodiac	Green, red, gold; Christmas trees and decorations
Traditional activities	Lion and dragon dance in a parade	Attend mass or some form of carol service to remember Christ's birth
Kinship	Being with family takes a central role; visit relatives during the Spring Festival	Being with family takes a central role
Wishes	Hope, prosperous, commercialism	Hope, prosperous, commercialism
Importance	The biggest human migration; millions leave the cities on trains, planes, and buses to get to their families in the countryside.	Different in degree

(2) 在理解了表层的文化现象后,请同学们分析这两个节日背后文化存在差异的原因。由于该问题的答案在文化背景和词汇掌握上的要求较高,在练习

前请同学们观看一个关于圣诞节的视频，练习设计为 half-guided practice，要求同学们将列出来的词汇填入表格。

Questions：

Why do the two festivals have so many differences?

Roman origin   Agrarian origin

Religious   Ancestor worship

Celebrate the return of the sun   Celebrate the start of spring

	Religion	Origin	Belief	Concept	Story
Spring Festival					
Christmas					

（3）引导同学们提取出两个节日的相同之处。

What are the similarities of the two festivals?

Family reunion

Sending good wishes

Promote the same concept of love, peace, and prosperity

Activity：

Make a Spring Festival card and Christmas card and ask the students who they want to give the cards to.

（4）请同学们分组讨论。

①问题一（促进自我文化身份认知）：Why do people need festivals?
同学们的回答包括：

For ordinary people：

Festivals are the soul of cultural and social life.

They teach us values and bring humans together.

Each and every celebration has its history and valid reasons.

Each festival has its interesting story.

Festivals bring freshness to life.

They remove boredom.

They are the source of national integration and unity.

They remind us of our cultural values.

They are good for an integrated nation and its unity.

We know who we are.

For a country：

Many people get employment.

Because of the celebration，the country's economy also develops.

For business：

Companies get profits by selling festival related products.

Tourism develops because some of the traditional events.

②问题二（促进批判思维形成）：Should we cancel some of the festivals?

③问题三（意识到文化的交流和尊重）：Why do festivals spread to other cultures?

Why do foreign people come to China to experience our Chinese Spring Festival?

Why do we want to know some other festivals in other countries?

Experience:（Mexico piñata）

Introduction of a new festival from Mexico.

Group work: hit piñata.

Questions:

How do you feel after taking part in the activity?

How do you think this activity and knowledge will help you in the future?

④问题四（深入对自身文化的理解）：How to make Spring Festival more popular among young people?

五、课程反思

节日是文化的集中体现，传承自己的节日文化就是守住自己的文化身份，我们需要了解自己的节日文化来建立文化自信和文化认同。世界上每种文化都有自己的特点并传承了自己的历史，我们也需要在充分理解和认同自身文化的基础之上去了解和尊重他国文化，这样才能更好地进行国际交流。

学生反馈：

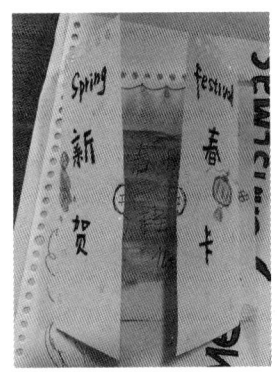

"我在国际理解课上了解了不同国家节日的相同和不同之处,知道了每种文化都有自己独特的历史和意义,都同样值得尊重。我认为文化交流的方式是守住自己的文化节日,知道自己是谁,再去了解和尊重别的国家的文化,促进文化的交流。"

"国家之间的节日文化的传播是不可避免的,我们应该在各种文化和节日交融的今天守住我们中国的传统节日,使我们的节日文化能够延续。"

分辨视角篇

课案五

探索自己的价值观

课程设计教师：

魏敏

成都树德中学国际部英语教师兼班主任

英国杜伦大学 英语教育硕士

曾在剑桥大学跟随知名作家 Derek Niemann 进修一年创意写作

荣获第四届"黑布林英语阅读"全国优课大赛一等奖

荣获四川省教育厅四川师范大学基础教育课程研究中心 2021 英语学科"整本书阅读"说课比赛一等奖

内容：

一、教学对象分析

二、教学内容

三、教学目标

四、教学方法

五、教学过程

六、作业布置

七、教学亮点

八、教学反思

一、教学对象分析

本堂课的教学对象是普通高中高二的学生，普高同学备战高考压力大，大部分时间用在刷题上，对自己的未来规划很模糊，等高考分数出来填志愿的那几天才开始考虑学校、专业的选择，但此时已来不及进行深入的思考和系统的规划。回想当年笔者自己在高考填报志愿的时候，无人指导，更不知道自己想要做什么，那时候多希望有一位老师能指点迷津。已为人师的我，不希望学生们再"患职业规划上的近视"，只看到高考，而忽视思考高考后更广阔的人生。

二、教学内容分析

本次的教学内容为探索自己的价值观。价值观对人们自身行为的定向和调节具有非常重要的作用。价值观决定人的自我认知，它直接影响和决定一个人的理想、信念、生活目标和追求方向的性质。但是价值观的概念对学生来说较为抽象，因此通过概念讨论、案例分析、方法实操一步步地从抽象到具体，从理论到实践，让同学们挖掘出自己的价值观，对自己的内心有更清楚的认识，从而在高考后选大学、专业的时候，能够做出更符合自己价值观的选择，从而有更浓厚的兴趣和更强烈的信念，把大学专业学好、学精。

三、教学目标

（1）理解价值观的概念。
（2）识别知名人物和知名组织的价值观，思考这些价值观对知名人物和知名组织的行为产生了什么影响。
（3）评判自我的价值观。
（4）分析个体价值观的成因，学会尊重不同人和不同组织的价值观。

四、教学方法

案例分析法、小组讨论法、探究学习法。

五、教学过程

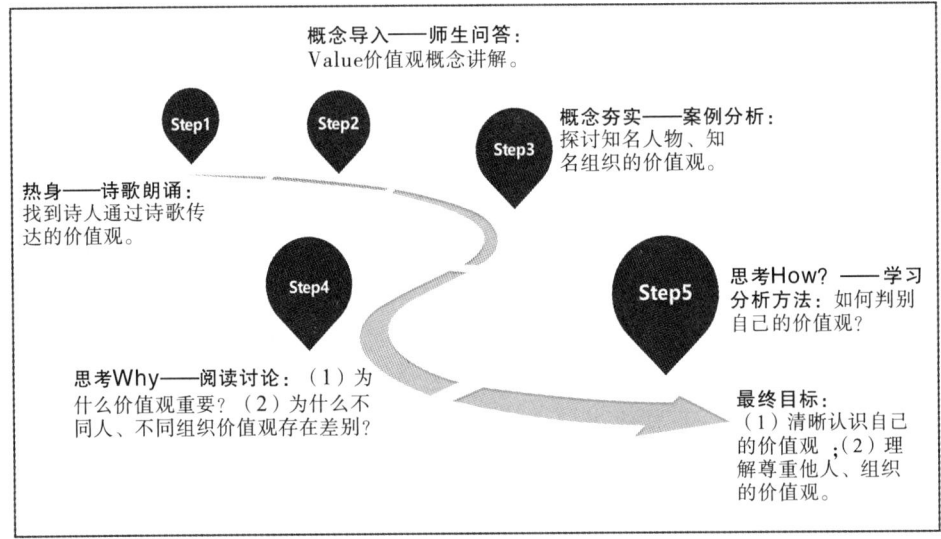

1. 热身——诗歌朗诵：找到诗人通过诗歌传达的价值观

Q: Which value does the poet treasure the most?

Liberty and love
These two I must have.
For my love I'll sacrifice
My life.
For liberty I'll sacrifice
My love.

— Petofi Sandor (Hungarian Poet)

匈牙利诗人 Petofi Sandor 关于"爱情，生命和自由"一诗

在课堂上，教师首先在电视大屏上呈现一首诗歌，给学生 3 分钟时间讨论诗歌和准备自由朗诵，然后请一位同学有感情地朗诵本诗。学生朗诵完毕，教师给予点评，并接着提问该同学：诗人认为"爱情""生命"和"自由"哪一项最重要？然后，再随机抽问别的同学。

最后，大家经过讨论，一致认为诗人认为"自由"最重要。教师点出这里的"自由"是诗人的价值观。接下来，教师继续抛出两个问题：

（1）同学们，你们认为"爱情""生命"和"自由"哪一个最重要呢？为什么？

（2）为什么大家的意见各不相同？谁的看法是正确的呢？

教师点出，这里的"什么更重要"其实就是价值观的体现，若想解答以上两个问题，同学们需进一步认识价值观。

2. 概念导入——师生问答：价值观（Value）概念讲解

在引起同学们的思考后，教师提问：什么是价值观？同学们分小组讨论，然后小组代表各抒己见。最后，教师给出一个价值观的概念，并请一位同学朗读。

"价值观"的概念

3. 概念夯实——案例分析：探讨知名人物、知名组织的价值观

在同学们对"价值观"有了概念性的理解后，可以开始探索国外名人的价值观，如迪士尼公司的创始人 Walt Disney、南非前总统 Nelson Mandela。两位名人来自不同行业，价值观也大不相同，但是他们都对社会做出了杰出贡献。教师提示同学们在思考的时候，从名人的行为、事件出发，因为价值观会指导人们的选择和行为，那反过来，观察一个人的选择和行为以及做出的重要事件，也能倒推出这个人的价值观。

Walt Disney 的价值观

What does he value?

Nelson Mandela

Equality

Nelson Mandela 的价值观

讨论完之后，教师从人再过渡到组织，进而了解组织的价值观，如企业、公益组织、学校等。同分析人的价值观一样，我们也可以从组织的文化、所从事的事业、提供的产品和服务等，去思考组织的价值观。此外，组织的价值观也深受其建立者和领导者的影响。

What does the company value?

- Innovation
- Diversity and inclusion
- Corporate social responsibility
- Philanthropies
- Environment
- Trustworthy computing

微软公司的价值观

在微软公司的价值观中，值得注意的是"Philanthropies"（慈善）一项，

分辨视角篇　055

这烙有微软创始人比尔·盖茨深深的印记。比尔及梅琳达·盖茨基金会成立于 2000 年，其致力于将人类的创新才能应用于减少健康和发展领域的不平等现象。2020 年 1 月 27 日，盖茨基金会提供 500 万美元紧急赠款，并提供相应的技术和专家支持，用于帮助中国相关合作伙伴加速在新型冠状病毒感染的流行病学、应急干预实施和医药产品研发等方面的工作。

What does the company value?

- 以客户为中心，以奋斗者为本
- 长期艰苦奋斗
- 坚持自我批判

华为公司的价值观

华为公司的狼性文化和自我批判精神，都是华为公司价值观的体现。

在看了两家杰出的 IT 公司的价值观后，我们可以发现华为公司同微软公司的价值观差别较大。虽然两家公司的价值观差别大，但是两者都成了当今世界上一流的 IT 企业。

What does the company value?

Be your good neighbor.

成都知名连锁超市红旗超市的价值观

成都知名连锁超市红旗超市的价值观:"红旗连锁,您的好邻居。"

What does Shude value?
Who set the value for Shude?

- Loyalty
- Courage
- Diligence

树德中学的价值观

接着思考母校的价值观,树德中学的价值观:"忠,勇,勤。"

4. 思考 Why——阅读讨论:为什么价值观重要

那价值观为什么重要呢?下面请阅读文章"Eight Benefits for Identifying

Your Values", 并思考识别自己价值观的重要性。

Eight Benefits for Identifying Your Values

What does the word "value" mean to you? Can you define it?

Values are what you believe matter most in life. Everyone's values are different. Some common values are love, success, friendship, intelligence, and respect.

As children, our parents and teachers pass values on to us and we live our lives based on what they've taught us is important, be that kindness, friendship, listening, etc. But as adults we must determine what is of most value to us on our own. Some of the values from childhood may stay the same, but you may realize that others have become increasingly more important as you have grown and changed. Tolerance, gratitude, and family, for example, may be of huge significance to you now.

So, without further ado, here are 8 benefits of identifying your values.

1. Values help you find your purpose.

Have you already figured out the purpose of life? If not, as is the case for most of us, values can help answer the all-encompassing question, "What is my purpose in life?" You can't expect to know what you want out of life if you don't know what is important in life. Knowing what you value gets you that much closer to an answer. Think about it.

2. Values help you react in difficult situations.

Values are guiding principles for behaviour. They can help ensure you behave in a way that matches who you want to be at your core. People often react quickly in situations, especially difficult ones, and they don't always take the time to think about what they are doing before they do it. You can use your values to reflect on situations, too, to decide, for example, if you need to apologize for something. What a helpful little tool!

3. Values help you make decisions.

When you come across the need to make a decision, your values can help you make the right call. Sometimes emotions get in the way of good decision making, but if you stop to ask yourself, "What would someone who values X do in this situation?" then you just might be able to come to a more clearheaded, less emotionally-affected decision.

4. Values help clear out clutter.

Do you ever want to eliminate excess baggage from your life? Identifying your values will help you rule out the things you really do not want, need or believe are important. People are consumed with so much these days. Weed the time-wasting things out of your life!

5. Values help you choose the right career.

All career paths come with pros and cons, we know that. But when you know what matters most to you, you can be sure you are choosing the right career path. If you value connection, interaction, and friendship, for example, then it's possible a work-at-home job may not be a good fit for you. On the other hand, if you value travel, wealth, and conversation, then maybe a traveling sales job is perfect for you. Sometimes knowing your values can even help you determine if a promotion is the best idea for you. Who knew saying no to a promotion could be a good idea?

6. Values help you develop a sense of self.

Knowing your values means you can develop strong opinions about important subjects. You don't want to just believe what your parents believed. You can't just say you believe what your friends believe. You need to figure out what you truly believe, and then you can share your honest self with others. This is important!

7. Values help increase your confidence.

Identifying your values increases your level of confidence because it brings about a sense of stability and safety to your life. When you know what you want, it doesn't matter what other people want. When you know what is important to you, it doesn't matter what is important to other people. This will naturally bring a sense of confidence to your life.

8. Values help your overall happiness level.

If you combine the results from benefits one through seven, then you have likely improved your life. You've developed a purpose, reacted better in difficult situations, made good decisions, found the right career, developed opinions, and increased your confidence. It's fair to say you might just feel a little happier!

阅读过后,请同学们思考以下问题:

(1) 你赞同识别价值观有这些好处吗?请举例说明自己的观点。

(2) 除此之外,识别清楚自己的价值观还有别的好处吗?

5. 思考How——分析学习:如何判别自己的价值观

以下为课堂阅读材料"Your Values, Your Life"。

"Your Values, Your Life"

Your values form the foundation of your life. They dictate the choices you make and determine the direction that your life takes. Your values will influence decisions related to your relationships, career, and other activities you engage in. Despite this importance, few people choose their values. Instead, they simply adopt the values of their parents and the dominant values of society. In all likelihood, the values that you internalized as a child remain with you through adulthood. Unfortunately, these values may also have created a life that is carrying you down a path that is not the direction you want to go at this point in your life.

What were the values you were raised with? What values are you presently living in accordance with? Are they the same or different? Do your values bring you happiness?

Deconstructing your values. To truly understand what values you possess and live by, you must deconstruct them until you are able to clearly see what exactly you value and why you hold those values. Looking openly and honestly at the way you were raised is the first step in identifying the values that you were instilled growing up. What did your parents value and what values did they impress upon you—achievement, wealth, education, religion, status, independence, appearance? Think back to your childhood and ask yourself several questions: What values were emphasized in the way your parents lived their lives? What values were stressed in your family? What values were reflected in the way you were rewarded or punished? For example, were you rewarded for being highly ranked in your high school class and for winning in sports, or were you rewarded for giving your best effort and for helping others?

Your next step in the deconstruction process involves looking at your present life and the values your life reflects. In responding to these questions, you should ask yourself what values underlie your answers. What do you do for a living—are you a corporate employee, a business owner, a teacher, a salesperson, a caterer, or a social worker? A common question that people in social gathering ask is: What do you do for a living? For example, though a bit of a generalization, it is probably safe to say that someone who becomes an investment banker has different values than someone who becomes an elementary school teacher. What those underlying values might be may vary, but one might assume that the investment banker values money, while the teacher values education and helping children. Where do you live? Do you live in a high-rise apartment in a city, in the suburbs, or in the country? And what values led you there? What activities do you engage in most—cultural, physical, religious, political, or social? And what values are reflected in those activities? What do you talk about mostly-politics, religion, economy, or other people? And what does that tell you about your values?

Finally, perhaps the most telling question reflecting what you value is: What do you spend your money on-a home, cars, travel, clothing, education, art, or charity? Because money is a limited resource for most people, they will use their money in ways that they value most. Over and above what people say and other indicators in their life, where they spend their hard-earned money says the most about their values. You can then ask yourself whether your current values are the same as those you grew up with. Have you gone through a period of examination and reconsideration? Have you consciously chosen to discard some values from your upbringing and adopt new ones? Now that you have deconstructed your life and have a clear idea of what you value, you can see the values upon which you have created your life. You can see whether those values contribute to your dissatisfaction or bring you happiness. Look at which aspects of your life contribute to your unhappiness—your career, marriage, or lifestyle? And ask yourself what values underlie those parts of your life.

阅读完毕后，请各小组思考并讨论以下问题：

（1）*According to the author, how do values affect human being? Whose values do humans usually take on?*

（2）*How many steps will you need to deconstruct your values? What are they?*

（3）*Do you agree or disagree with the following statement? People simply adopt the values of their parents and the dominant values of society.*

Three steps to deconstruct your values

Step 1: Look openly and honestly at the way you were raised

Step 2: Consider your future career path
Ask yourself: How will your future house look like?
What activities do you engage in the most?

Step 3: Think about this question: What will you spend your money on?

六、作业布置

（1）小组作业。思考关于"爱情，生命和自由"一诗的作者匈牙利诗人Petofi Sandor为什么认为"自由"最重要。同学们需要调查诗人的成长环境和成长经历，通过调研论证自己的答案，并制作PPT在课堂上汇报。

（2）就"我们如何理解和对待价值观的多样性？"写一篇500字的英文文章。

七、教学亮点

本课程的教学亮点包括：

（1）从理论到实践，让同学们从理解抽象概念，到能够用具体的方法判别自己的价值观。

（2）选取积极正面、覆盖面广的案例，学生除了从案例中学习价值观，还能对感兴趣的案例进行更深入的研究。

（3）概念本土化，将对价值观的理解带入成都人熟知的红旗超市中，带入校园和班级中。同学们能够将所学知识运用到生活中，养成关爱身边人、关注身边事的习惯，成为用心的、善于观察的学习者。

八、教学反思

本课程的深度还有待提高，对于如何引导学生探索、建立自己较为系统的价值观，教师和学生都需要在阅读和实践中投入更多的思考。

此外，笔者主要从事国际高中教育，对于目前国内普通高中学生的学情和需求仍需进一步了解。

课案六

性别思维定式
——赋能学生　主动学习

课程设计教师：

吴洁

树德国际部英语教师

美国普渡大学教育学硕士研究生

曾任教于新加坡国际学院，进修于新加坡管理大学

曾任 ASIC 英国学术鉴定委员会下新加坡国际学院学术委员会委员

参与新加坡私立教育理事会 CPE 的文化及学术交流

TESOL 认证国际英语教师

IB English B 执教资格认证

内容：

一、课程概念

二、学习方式

三、课程理论

四、课程活动

五、课程亮点

六、课程实施

七、课程反思

一、课程概念

关于国际理解课程,笔者一直在思考一连串的问题:为什么要教这门学科?通过这门学科的教学,能够让学生掌握哪些知识和技能?除了掌握的知识和技能以外,还能拓展哪些额外的内容给学生?而教师又要采用什么样的教学方式、方法去实践自己的想法?

全球胜任力,这是笔者对以上所有问题给出的答案。笔者清晰地认识到自己的授课目标:要培养出具有全球胜任力的人,一个走出学校后有能力在世界舞台上有所建树的群体。

传统的课堂大都由教师主导和控制,学生的互动和参与都受到了压制。无趣、刻板、不生动等弊端也一直被家长及社会各方所质疑。在这种教学模式中,日复一日地进行类似内容的重复教学,教师的主观能动性也受到了很大限制。缺少创新、按部就班的工作模式也让教师逐渐在工作中失去激情。因此,发挥主观能动性,不断地对教学方法和教学理论进行创新成为教师保持教学活力的重要部分。

综上,在这节关于性别定式的课堂里,笔者主要采取学生主动学习的教学方式。

二、学习方式——主动学习的魅力

"Active Learning"中文译作"主动学习",也可译作"自主学习",这是以学生为中心的一种学习过程,鼓励学生主动思考而非被动接受教师传递的信息,其关注学生"如何学习"(How),而非"学了什么"(What)。简而言之,Active Learning 就是在教师的引导下让学生的思维动起来。既然是激发学生思维的跳动,学习便不受空间的限制。

美国学者埃德加·戴尔在 1946 年提出"学习金字塔"理论,美国国家训练实验室关于学习金字塔的研究结果表明,Active Learning 在教学中的应用将大大增加学习内容的留存率,有助于教学效率及学习效果的提升。从下图中我们可以通过数字了解到,采用不同的学习方式,学习者在两周以后能记住的内容(平均学习留存率)有巨大的差异。

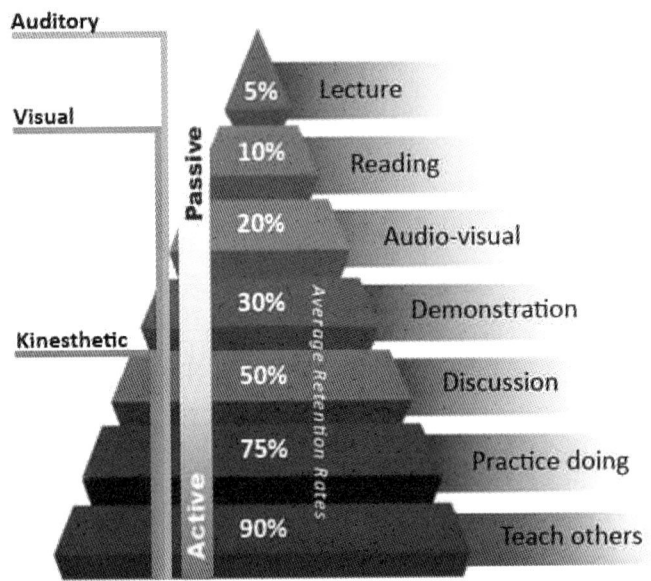

埃德加·戴尔把学习效率分为七个层次。

第一层次,讲授。

讲授就是听讲,就是用听的方法进行学习,使用此方法的学习效率是最差的,如学生听教师讲课、听录音、听广播等,都属于这种方法。经过24个小时,学生只能学到教师所讲内容的5%。

这个方法可能是很多学校里使用最多的方法,学生在学校的大部分时间都是在听教师讲课。另外,在教师上课过程中,有些学生的注意力还不集中,其学习效果也就可想而知了。

第二层次,阅读。

阅读也是我们最常用的学习方法,像看书、看报、看手机上的文章都属于这种方法,这种方法的学习效率也很低,其平均学习留存率只有10%。

第三层次,声音图片。

这种方法在现在的教学中已经比较常用,如视频教学、教师边讲边放图片等。这种方法的学习留存率为20%,虽然效率也比较低,但比听和看的效果明显要好一些。

第四层次,示范演示。

示范演示更多是用于操作性内容的学习,如学习开车、做饭、修理等。这种方法不太适用于纯理论性知识的学习,而学生的学习大多属于理论性知识的学习。这种方法的学习留存率为30%。

第五层次，小组讨论。

这种方法的学习留存率可以达到 50%。但是在现实课堂中，真正应用这种方法的教师不是太多。

第六层次，实际演练，做中学。

这种方法的学习留存率可以达到 75%，这就要求学生亲自参与到学习中去，自己去实践，在实践中学习。如学生做作业、写作、在操作性学习中自己动手等。

第七层次，训练他人。

训练他人就是给他人当老师，把自己学习到的知识讲授给别人。这种学习方法的留存率最高，可以达到 90%。因为你如果要去给别人当老师，自己必须将所要教的内容彻底掌握。

三、课程理论——建构主义学习理论

主动学习教学理论源于 20 世纪 80 年代兴起的建构主义学习理论（Constructivism），瑞士著名心理学家让·皮亚杰（Jean Piaget）因其创立的儿童认知发展理论，被看作是当代建构主义理论的最早提出者。建构主义学习理论有两个重要的观点：第一，学习者是主体，学习者是有自己的知识经验的，没有背景知识作基础、超过学生的认知去教学是无效的。教学要尊重儿童原有知识经验的丰富性，并将其作为新知识的生长点，引导儿童从原有的知识经验中"生长"出新的知识经验。即教师应重视学生对各种现象的理解，倾听他们的意见，洞察他们的想法的由来，并以此为根据，引导学生丰富或调整自己的理解。教师应充分认识儿童原有经验背景的差异，学生对问题的理解常常有差异，而学生经验世界的差异本身就是一种宝贵的学习资源。教学就是要增进学生之间的合作，促使学生在一个学习的共同体中相互沟通、合作、分享，使更多学生个体看到那些与他不同的观点，从而对问题形成更丰富的、多角度的理解（真正学习的发生）。第二，学习是一种高度社会化的行为。学习不能孤军奋战、只在一个个大脑中发生。教师和学生、学习者之间，需要针对某些问题一起进行探索、交流、讨论，甚至质疑，形成"学习共同体"，在一个社会情境中去学习。知识是不可能脱离活动情境而抽象存在的，学习应该与情境化的社会实践活动结合起来。

四、课程活动

1. Think-Pair-Share

其实融入新的教学模式并不需要花大力气去对整个课堂进行调整，只需要从加入一些主动教学的元素开始。

教师通常可以在引入新话题时采用 Think-Pair-Share 的方式，用时建议 5~10 分钟。

（1）教师可抛出一个问题或者提出一个观点，学生先自己思考要怎么回答或者反馈，也可以写下自己的答案，用时 2 分钟左右。（Think）

（2）学生跟自己旁边的一位同学组成一组，互相说出自己的回答或者观点，用时 2~3 分钟。（Pair）

（3）教师给出停止讨论的信号，然后请一些小组的同学与全班同学分享他们的回答或者观点，用时 5 分钟左右。（Share）

最后，教师将大家在 Think-Pair-Share 活动中讨论、分享出来的内容跟将要继续学习的内容衔接起来，顺利过渡。

以下是笔者在这堂课里对 Think-Pair-Share 的实际操作。

第一个教学活动是让学生画出他们印象中的科学家。这个想法来源于著名的科学家形象绘画测验（Draw-a-Scientist Test）。20 世纪 60—70 年代，社会学家大卫·钱伯斯（David Chambers）邀请来自加拿大和美国的近 5000 名幼儿园到小学五年级的孩子来画一位科学家。结果发现，在这些画中，只有 28 幅画是女性科学家，仅占全部的 0.6%，且这 28 幅全都是女生画的。几乎所有儿童画出的科学家都是穿着实验服、戴眼镜并留有胡子的男性科学家。

这个测验打破了语言、文字甚至文化的障碍，被之后的研究者广泛应用，成为研究科学家形象的经典方案。而长久以来的研究表明，科学家在学生心目中的"男性化"倾向非常严重，这说明学生对职业性别角色的意识受到了社会期待的影响。这也可能是女性进入 STEM 领域（科学、技术、工程和数学）的人数远远低于男性的原因之一。

不出意料的是，全班共 25 位同学画的全部是男性科学家，如下图所示。

在这个环节中，教师抛出以下三个话题，学生 5 人为一个小组开始 Think－Pair－Share 环节。

What were the similarities and differences among the drawings?
Why do you think those similarities exist among our drawings?
What did you learn by doing this?

2. Cooperative Learning

在美国课堂有一种深受推崇和流行的教学方法——合作学习结构法（Kagan Cooperative Learning）。合作学习结构法是由史宾塞·卡甘（Spencer Kagan）提出的，他曾是美国加利福尼亚大学心理学和教育学教授，现主要负责有关合作学习结构教学材料的出版和合作学习的教师培训工作。

自 1968 年以来，卡甘博士致力于合作学习结构的研究，目前已经设计开发出 200 多种步骤明确并简单易学的合作结构游戏。学生之间相互依赖，并且共同参与到学习活动中。每个人在合作学习的活动中都有平等的参与机会，但也有每个人独立的任务和责任。卡甘博士的合作学习不仅只考量小组的综合成绩，也会给突出的个人额外的奖励。

想要搭建小组合作学习的环境，需要哪些要素呢？卡甘博士提出有七大要素是实现学生合作学习的关键，它们分别是：合作学习结构游戏（教学策略）、团队、课堂管理、教室建设、团队建设、社交技巧、基本原理。掌握了合作学习结构游戏和团队建设就可以开启简单的合作学习的课堂。

（1）合作学习结构游戏。

卡甘博士设计了很多教学游戏，而这些游戏只有框架结构，没有具体内容，教师可以根据这个框架搭建任何想要的内容。

比如，现在你拥有一个爱心形状的模具，你倒入巧克力，它就变成一个爱心巧克力；如果你倒入的是布丁，它就成了一个爱心布丁。转换到教学上，教师可以将这个教学游戏框架应用于语文课、数学课、编程课等，即"内容+结构=活动"，将不同的内容与结构相搭配就生成不同的教学活动，而一系列不同的课程活动组合在一起就成了一节课。

卡甘博士已经开发出 200 多种合作学习的结构游戏，可以让合作学习课堂变得非常有趣，学生不会觉得千篇一律、枯燥重复。有一个叫"Four Corners"（四个角落）的结构游戏，在此游戏中没有对错，大家只是在分享自己的观点，所以大家可以选择自己喜欢的观点。比如，教室的四个角落分别贴着 1、2、3、4 的数字，四个数字下分别有不同风格的服装。学生选择自己喜欢的服装风格并移动到那个角落，他们可以和同样喜欢这个服装风格的同学互相交流为什么喜欢这个风格。最后，教师会请同学们在全班进行分享。

合作教学的教学策略有很多，在这堂课中笔者主要采取了合作教学中一个叫"Jigsaw"（切块拼接法）的教学方法。Jigsaw 是由阿伦森（Elliot Aronson）等人在 20 世纪 70 年代提出的一种合作学习方式，其本意是"拼图玩具"，即将一张完整的图案分成诸多小块，由游戏者按照一定的思路将其再拼接起来。Jigsaw 合作学习方式是把学习任务切割成几部分，然后再将部分任务整合的一种教学方法。学生想要掌握其他的学习内容，唯一的途径就是认真倾听其他小组成员的讲解。因而他们都具有相互支持的学习动机，并表现出对彼此作业的极大兴趣和关注，同时也提高了小组内部成员的独立性。

下面这张图展示了 Jigsaw 的主要元素。

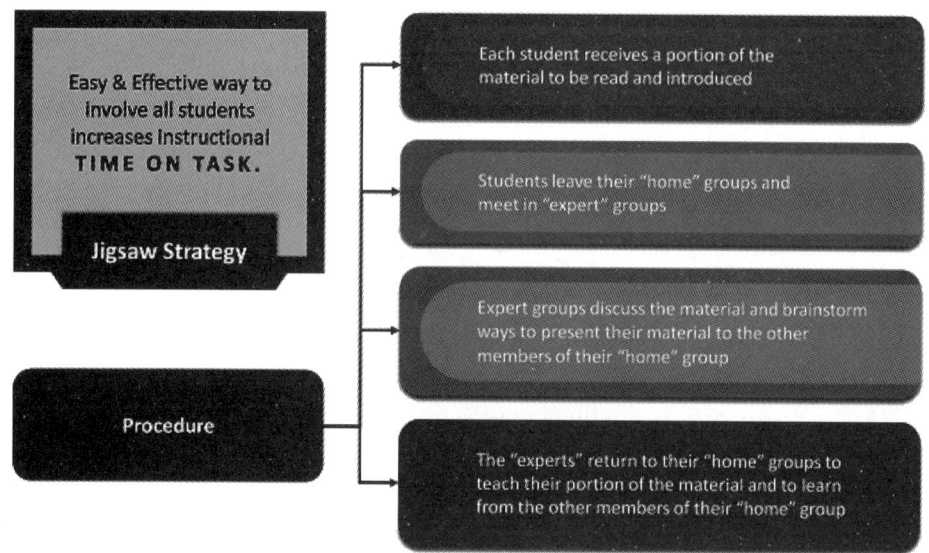

第一步：材料切分。将教学内容分成若干个片段，小组的每位同学领取一个片段任务。

第二步：专家交流。领取同一片段任务的同学组成专家组。

第三步：学习讨论。专家组学习研究资料，掌握内容，探讨将内容传授给原小组同学的方法。

第四步：知识拼接。"专家们"返回各自小组，教授组员，每位组员分享不同方面的内容。

（2）团队建设。

小组合作学习顾名思义就是由多个学生组成一个小组，小组内成员互相合作进行学习活动。这就必然会涉及如何将学生分为不同的小组。卡甘博士提出了四种不同的分组类型：同质组、异质组、随机组、兴趣组。

卡甘博士推荐四人一组，这样能在保证学习资源多样性的同时，展开两两配对活动，大大提高每个学生的参与度，真正做到公平参与。

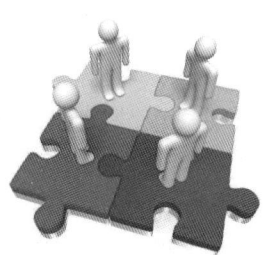

研究证明，当小组成员超过 4 人时，将会降低他们的参与程度，这样整个课堂的参与度和学生的学习

效率都会有所降低。

如果是一个20人的课堂，有1个学生被提问并回答问题，那么只有1/20的人在积极参与课堂活动。如果要让每个学生都分享自己的想法，每个人1分钟，则一共需要20分钟的时间。如果教师把课堂分为两个大组，每个组有10个人，并且允许每个小组成员在小组内发表自己的看法，那一共则需要10分钟的时间。小组规模过大，会降低合作效率，但合作小组的规模也并非越小越好，两人小组虽然会增加学生的互动，但思想的多元性和丰富性却会随之减少。当然在实际操作中，教师也要考虑实际学生人数来尽量合理安排。

3. Inquiry-Driven Learning

探究能够规划组织我们对未知事物的思考。在探究过程中，我们需要细心观察周围的环境，同时又要保持可创造性。在教育教学中，探究性学习（Inquiry-Driven Learning）是一种建构主义方法，学生能够通过提问、收集和分析信息，找到解决方案，做出决定和采取行动，从而拥有学习的所有权。

学生通过探究性学习认识到理解科学不仅仅是了解事实，还可以通过修改和完善现有的概念，来建立他们已知的知识，并形成新的知识。此外，学生在新环境下运用知识的能力也是基于学生学习理解的程度。这些优势使得学生学习的积极性变得越来越高。教师应鼓励学生实践，将新知识传授给他人，在小组中讨论，而不是简单地听教师讲课或仅仅通过自我阅读来学习。

探究性学习中最流行的就是项目式学习（Project-Based Learning），指学生在教师的辅导下，对真实、有趣和复杂的问题或挑战进行一段时间持续的调查研究，从而获得知识和技能。它是一种以学生为中心的教学方式。在学习过程中，学生会积极地收集信息、获取知识、探讨方案，以此来解决具有现实意义的问题。

还有一个笔者经常在教学中使用的探究式教学策略是 See-Think-Wonder。哈佛大学教育学院"零点计划"（Project Zero）有个历经几十年的研究项目，发现了一套"可视化思维"方法。

这三个步骤分别是：

I see（我看到了什么？）

I think（我想到了什么？）

I wonder（还有什么我想了解的或延伸到的？）

这是一套训练思考和学习能力的教学方式，已被广泛纳入美国中小学教学。教师可以用图片导入课堂，然后基于以上步骤设计关于该图片的问题。这个思考方式能够引导学生推理，从而想到一些之前没有想到的角度，帮助学生深入理解，激发学生的学习兴趣，培养学生善于思考和探究的能力。

以下是笔者将 Jigsaw 和 Inquiry-Driven Learning 融合在一起的实际操作。

第一步：准备。

One driving question for the lesson:

How can we create a community where people are free from the stereotyped gender roles?

笔者设计了五个 Essential Questions，每个 Essential Question 下设置了相应的阅读材料和阅读探索任务，然后将资料张贴在了教室的五个站点，这五个 Essential Questions 为：

How does media help build gender stereotypes?

How does language help build gender stereotypes?

How does family help build gender stereotypes?

How does sport help build gender stereotypes?

How does school help build gender stereotypes?

第二步：学生 5 人一组，小组的每位同学领取一个阅读任务。然后每组中领到相同任务的成员组成专家组。

第三步：学习讨论。专家组学习研究资料，掌握内容，探讨将内容传授给原小组同学的方法。

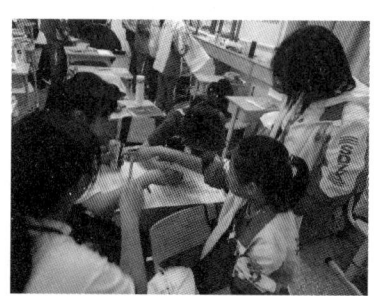

第四步：知识拼接。"专家们"返回各自小组，教授组员，每位组员分享不同的内容。

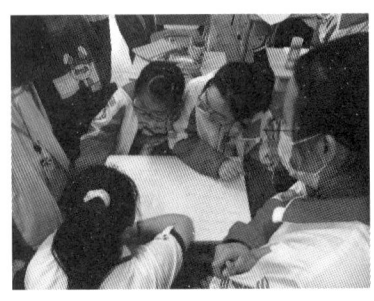

每一个问题的解答都能带来更多的问题，教育教学就变成了一个无限的游戏。

五、课程亮点：将科技融入教学

如果课堂里学生可以使用电脑或者平板、手机等设备的话，还可以融入一些科技元素，创造一个网络空间，以此促进课程的广度和深度。笔者比较推荐的线上互动软件是Padlet。Padlet是一个在线协作工具，只需要通过简单的拖拽式操作就可以很快做出一个属于自己的"故事墙"。

下图是笔者在自己的教学中使用的Padlet主题墙，引导学生围绕课程中的问题展开头脑风暴。学生可以在Padlet墙上看到别人的想法，也可以添加自己的想法。同学们可以在上面附上关于话题的链接。头脑风暴结束后，教师可以有针对性地对墙上的内容进行进一步的分析和讲解。

学生的想法往往会让老师意想不到。所以在头脑风暴的过程中，教师应该尽可能引导学生多发动奇思妙想，强调这是"头脑风暴时刻"，让学生有空间可发挥。

Padlet 还有很多其他的用处，比如，在 Padlet 里面建立一面"问题墙"，这样可以让那些不敢提问的学生通过匿名的方式把问题说出来，也可以让那些不知道如何问问题或是暂时还没有想到自己的问题的学生看到其他同学的问题，从而促进大家思考。此外，学生也可以建立在线小组，共同合作，查找资料或者撰写报告。小组成员可以在属于自己小组的"小组墙"内，把各自找到的资料贴到墙上去，也可以直接在墙上发布自己的想法和建议。Padlet 支持多种不同文件的上传，如图片、视频、文档、超链接等，小组成员还可以根据墙上不同帖子的内容，利用连接线来整理帖子之间的关系。Pandlet 还有一个强大的功能就是收集学生的作品，教师可以在课堂上把墙上的作品展示给大家观看，并且有针对性地进行点评，学生也可以在课后观看墙上的作品。这样既可以培养学生的分享精神，也可以在学生中形成良性的竞争关系，促进学生共同进步。

Padlet 是一个可以增加师生、生生之间互动的在线协作的好工具，灵活而恰当地运用它可以让课堂增色不少。

六、实施过程：项目式学习

在性别思维定式这个话题上，这个项目的 Essential Question 是：How can we debunk gender stereotype? 因此，本课程相应设置了一个创建网站的项目。

此项目要求整个班级创立一个网站来总结反思这个单元的内容，并且利用这个网站来分享学生对这个观点的理解，呼吁更多的人认识这个问题并且采取行动。通过建立网站，学生锻炼了探索解决问题的能力和团队合作沟通能力，同时也锻炼了利用现代科技产品解决问题的能力。

以下是团队合作分工表格,全班分为三个组,每个组承担不同的任务。

Task Category	Detailed Task	Group
Selecting a theme designing a website	visual effect navigation social media font and color	Group A
Preparing website content	prepare articlea writing essential content make a video design the quiz	Group B
Launching your website	create your account set up the pages upload the content test the website	Group C

在教师的指导下,同学们利用课外的时间从网站策划到最终建立,一共耗时一个月持续调查研究,获得了知识和技能。在这个探究的学习过程中,学生在小组中积极地收集信息、获取知识、探讨方案,以此来建立网站做宣传,教育周围社区的其他学生认识性别思维定式以及采取有效的措施来应对。

同学们设计的网站以六个 Learning Journey 展开,其中融入了阅读材料、同学们自己录制的视频、设计的问卷等元素。最终,我们就同学们设计的网站给出了结果报告。

网站部分截图如下。

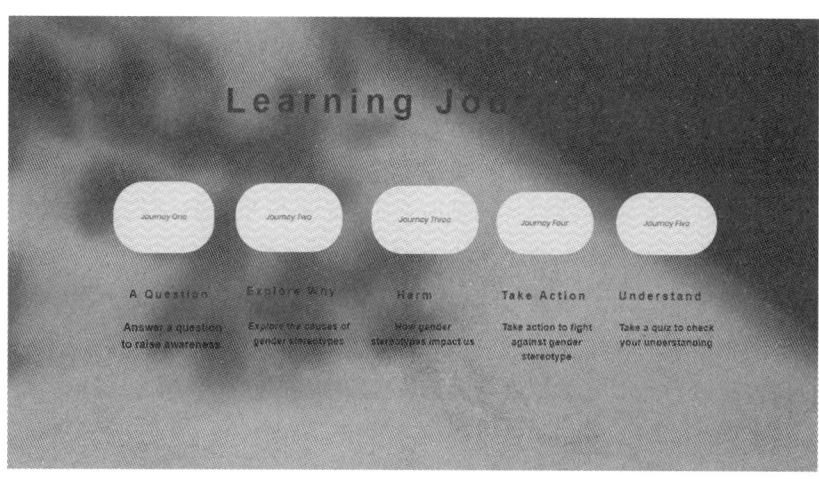

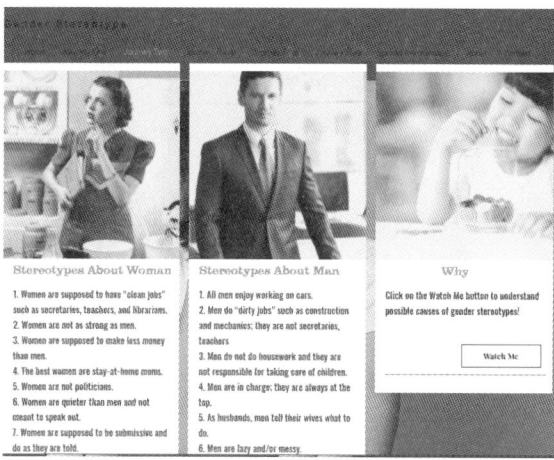

七、课程反思

正如卓越的教育家苏霍姆林斯基所言:"如果你想让教师的劳动能够给教师带来乐趣,使天天上课不至于变成单调乏味的义务,那就应当引导教师走上从事研究这条幸福之路上来。"作为教师,我们要不断探寻新的有效的教学理论和教学方法来帮助学生开阔眼界,培养他们的全球胜任力。只有具备全球胜任力的教师才能培养出有全球胜任力的学生。做个终身学习者,我们既是彼此的学生,也是彼此的老师。

课案七

不同文化对于想象力的影响

课程设计教师：
黄雨晴
四川大学英语语言文学硕士
获欧盟政府奖学金，访学比利时
6年国际教育教学经验
ETS 认证教师
IG global perspective 认证教师
内容：
一、课程背景
二、课程构思
三、课程目标
四、课程实施
五、课程反思

一、课程背景

当我们希望借着有限的智慧探究奥秘的时候，想象就成了必不可少的媒介。想象力作为连接过去、现在和未来的桥梁，在真实和虚幻之间创造了迷人的空间。我们每天运用想象力，透过现象探寻本质，也通过想象力逃离现实的桎梏，尽情描绘超越当下的未来。可以说，想象是创新的源泉，是无数艺术的缪斯。那么，想象作为一种认知的方式，一种了解世界、获取知识的方式，又是如何在不同文化中展示其深受该文化影响的面貌呢？

二、课程构思

国际理解课程基于上述思考，以想象力的展示载体之———艺术作品为切入点和讨论点，设计了一门探寻不同文化影响想象力的课程。该课程由定义想象力、判断文化对于想象力的影响因素、创作基于不同文化特征的作品、作品展示评估、课程反思回顾五个部分组成，希望这个课堂能让同学们更加了解想象力，了解不同文化对于想象力的影响，并能最终以运用想象力创作作品的形式加深对西方文化与东方文化的了解。

三、课程目标

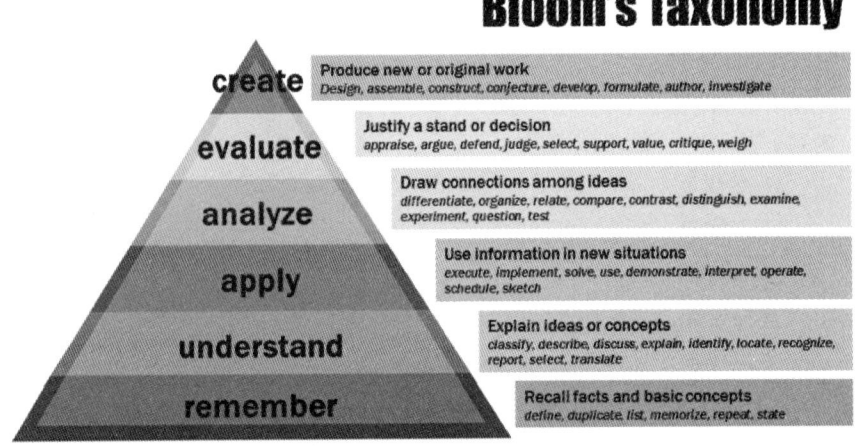

基于布鲁姆的学习认知理论，国际理解课堂希望学生不仅能够掌握一些知识信息，同时还能利用所获得的信息阐述与佐证自己的观点，最后进行基于课程理解的创作并展示。在想象力的课堂中，学生首先需要了解想象力的定义，阅读文本并总结文化对于想象力的影响；然后基于不同的文化特征，创作可以展示其特征的作品，以此达到学生对东西方文化的深入理解，激发学生的文化自信，并以更包容、尊重的态度对待其他文化。

知识目标：了解想象力的定义；了解不同文化的想象力特征。

技能目标：用文本寻找证据来佐证观点；运用不同材料展示自己的观点。
认知目标：增强学生的文化自信，以更包容的态度对待其他文化。

四、课程实施

基于上述的课程目标设置，该课程的内容由知识—技能—认知各部分层层推进。首先让学生通过 TED 视频的介绍来定义想象力，让学生知道何为想象力；然后由教师给出文本研究，让学生通过文本阅读了解文化对想象力的影响，并在讨论时找出文本证据；接着让学生基于课堂所学，进行不同主题的作品创作，并在课堂上用英文展示自己的作品，阐述作品理念；最后学生与教师进行课程反思。

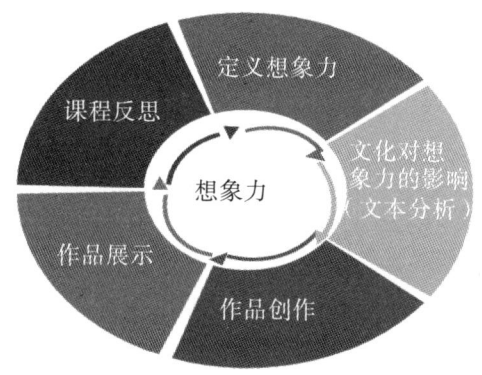

（一）定义想象力

在课堂引入部分，教师展示了一幅名为《想象》的画作，引导学生思考何为想象力，并要求学生在 5 分钟之内创作一幅以"想象"为主题的手绘作品，并总结想象力的特征。

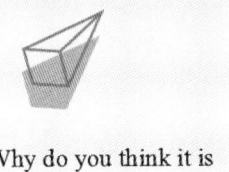

引入部分

学生作品

学生通过动手创作和思考总结出想象力的一些特点，如想象力是来源于现实世界中的感官体验；想象力是超脱于现实，着眼于未来的；想象力是人类创新的源泉。接着，教师展示了 TED 视频中对想象力特点和形成机制的介绍，加深了学生对想象力的理解，并由此得出想象力的定义。

视频截图

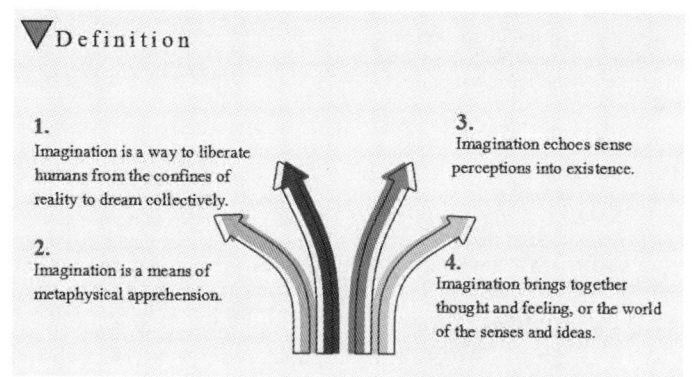

（二）判断文化对于想象力的影响因素

这一部分以想象力的一种表现形式——艺术作品为载体，探究文化对于想象力的影响究竟有哪些，又是如何作用在艺术作品上的。课堂上首先向学生展示了同一时期不同文化的雕塑形象（希腊、印度以及中国），学生需要判断这三组雕塑分别属于哪一个国家，并且给出判断依据。接下来，教师运用头脑风暴的方法让学生想象创作者在展示自己的想象力时可能受到了哪些因素的影响。

学生们在回答中给出了很多非常有意思的回答，如希腊靠海，所以其艺术作品总是很飘逸；又如古代中国等级制度森严，王权至上，所以多数作品强调规矩，没有太多个性的展现。

接着学生分为 3 个小组（小组角色课前已经分配好），教师分发不同的阅读资料，要求学生阅读后进行小组讨论，最后在全班展示论据和结果。

century art, not in terms of its use of symbols, but in terms of its significance as a *symbol itself*—a symbolic expression of the psychological condition of the modern world.

In the following pages, I have chosen three recurring motifs with which to illustrate the presence and nature of symbolism in the art of many different periods. These are the symbols of the stone, the animal, and the circle—each of which has had enduring psychological significance from the earliest expressions of human consciousness to the most sophisticated forms of 20th-century art.

Left, a prehistoric menhir—a rock that has been slightly carved into a female form (probably a mother goddess). Right, a sculpture by Max Ernst (born 1891) has also hardly altered the natural shape of the stone.

We know that even unhewn stones had a highly symbolic meaning for ancient and primitive societies. Rough, natural stones were often believed to be the dwelling places of spirits or gods, and were used in primitive cultures as tombstones, boundary stones, or objects of religious veneration. Their use may be regarded as a primeval form of sculpture—a first attempt to invest the stone with more expressive power than chance and nature could give it.

The Old Testament story of Jacob's dream is a typical example of how, thousands of years ago, man felt that a living god or a divine spirit was embodied in the stone and how the stone became a symbol:

And Jacob ... went toward Haran. And he lighted upon a certain place, and tarried there all night, because the sun was set; and he took of the stones of the place, and put them for his pillows and lay down in that place to sleep. And he dreamed, and behold a ladder set up on the earth, and the top of it reached to heaven, and behold the angels of God ascending and descending on it. And, behold, the

Among the many sects and movements that arose about A.D. 1000, the alchemists played a very important part. They exalted the mysteries of matter and set them alongside those of the "heavenly" spirit of Christianity. What they sought was a wholeness of man encompassing mind and body, and they invented a thousand names and symbols for it. One of their central symbols was the *quadratura circuli* (the squaring of the circle), which is no

more than the true mandala.

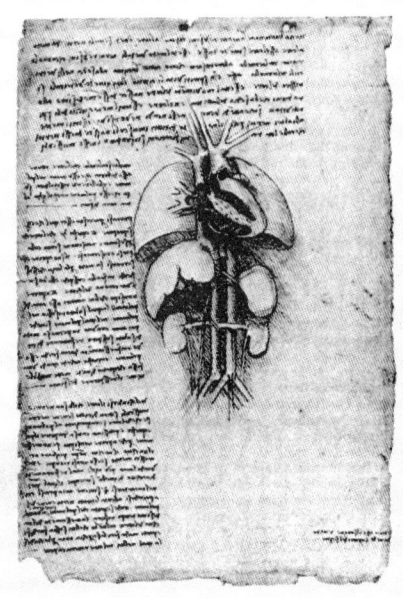

部分阅读资料

The influence of a culture on imagination

Your group:

Influence	Evidence from the reading
1	
2	
3	

Other group:

Influence	Evidence from the reading
1	
2	
3	
4	
5	

小组讨论以及展示时所用表格

学生在阅读、讨论和展示之后，更深刻地理解了文化对于想象力的影响。一种文化所处的地理位置、气候、盛行的价值观念与行事风格，都会使想象力呈现出巨大的不同，形成独特的文化景象。当了解到文化与想象力之间的这一层关系后，想象力便不再是天马行空、不受任何约束的认知方式，相反，它被文化之绳牵引着，在自由与偶然中寻出一种必然，一种由文化影响的必然。

（三）创作基于不同文化特征的作品

在本堂课之前，学生已经学习过文艺复兴时期的艺术特征和中国传统艺术特征。因此，本次课程要求学生以西方文化特征或东方文化特征为主题，选取其中一个特点并运用想象力创作一幅作品，形式不限。在作品创作完成之后，学生在班里进行展示，教师会按照作品的内容以及学生展示时所表现出来的专业程度进行打分。

criteria / candidate	Topic	Content	PPT	English Skill	Presentation Skill	Activity	Time Management	Overall Score
	novel, interesting, positive and in-depth	in-depth, demonstrate logically and clearly	clear, logical and beautiful	good pronunciation, vocabulary, grammar, intonation, fluency and coherence	appropriate body language, gestures and facial expressions	proper interaction with audience	present around 10 minutes	
	0-5	0-35	0-15	0-20	0-10	0-10	0-5	
1								
2								
3								
4								
5								
6								

Presentation Evaluation Form　　　Date:＿＿＿＿＿＿

同学们拿到作业任务之后，纷纷开动脑筋，大家课后讨论、线上询问、组团考察博物馆等，忙得不亦乐乎。两个星期之后，每个人都带着自己心仪的"作品"站上讲台进行展示。

（四）作品展示评估

在这一阶段，学生们除了拿出"作品"惊艳四座外，还有一个很重要的部分是如何运用演说的技巧向教师和同学们传达作品的设计理念、内容以及思想。在展示过程中，学生的PPT制作、英语表达、身体语言、观众互动和时间管理等都会纳入考察范畴。

部分学生的展示现场

学生们的表现无疑是优秀的。一位同学把《最后的晚餐》和13位帝王的形象完美结合,创造了"帝王的晚餐";一位同学运用黑色、粉色、橘色、白色抽象地展示了文艺复兴时期从神到人的思维转换;一位同学选取"鲤跃龙门"和"后羿射日"的中国神话传说,在画作中创造了一个龙与太阳战斗的场面;还有一位同学通过爬虫抓取的数据色块来直接对比同一时期中国和欧洲的不同画作与人们的思想,非常具有创新性。

部分同学的作品

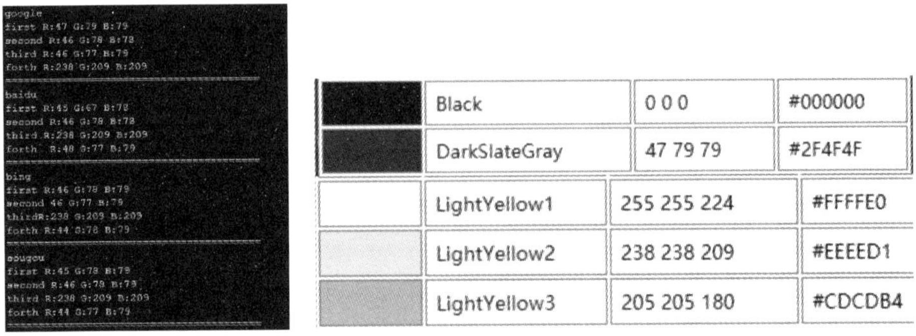

某同学的创作过程

（五）同学课后反思

L同学的发言："通过这堂想象力及其与文化的关系的课，我更加了解了文化的巨大影响，并由此更深刻了解到一些现象背后的文化根源。课堂后的作业本身也是想象力的极大展现。在拿到老师给的题目之后，我第一时间想到的是让观众参与创作的过程。但是通过绘画等传统艺术很难让观众代入，所以我选择了我最擅长的方式：数据。我从年份、内容、品种等几个品类中选择了最容易搜集、分析，也最容易看出差别的——颜色。随后，我用代码对网上关于文艺复兴和同时期中国的画作进行了搜集以及分类，然后将数据进行总结就得出了整个文艺复兴时期中西画作的不同特点。最后，我用装置艺术的形式展示了我搜集到的数据。在整个创作过程中，我发现东西方文化的差异真的不小。我开始认识到我们的言行和观念受到文化的影响如此之大，这也就不难理解为什么东西方对很多问题的解释会展示出完全不同的思路。"

五、课程反思

这一堂课以想象力的展示载体之一——艺术作品为切入点和讨论点，探寻不同文化如何影响想象力。在定义想象力的部分，通过学生自己创作、观看视频和身体活动，理解了想象力究竟是什么。在判断文化对想象力的影响的部分，通过图片引入以及材料阅读，一方面让学生对文化与想象力的关系有了更深入的了解，另一方面也训练了学生在英语阅读中寻证总结的能力，不同的阅读材料能够保证每一个小组的分享都是"新"的，避免了一些课堂活动中未分享小组无事可做的情况。在创作环节，教师给学生两周的课后时间去完成作品,并在班级群里定期询问进度以及解答相关疑问,给予适当指导,使得学生能在最大限度内发挥自己的想象力。最后在作品展示评估部分,学生需要展现出对作品的深刻理解以及适当的演讲技巧,用精准的语言表达作品中蕴含的文化主题。

  这课堂希望借由这个课题让同学们更加了解想象力,了解不同文化对于想象力的影响,进而更深刻地理解其他文化。了解不同的文化视角,表达自己也理解他人。唯愿在这种相互理解中,人类命运共同体能够真正实现。

课案八

多变量微积分在国内外的应用

课程设计教师：
陈俊名

拥有多年国际教育经验，遵循以人为本，以兴趣为导向的教学风格；融教育于文化，添思维于课堂，实现思维能力和学习能力的双提升。

内容：
一、课程背景
二、课程简介
三、课程结构
四、课程实例展示
五、课程亮点
六、课程反思

一、课程背景

作为一名人民教师，我们肩负的使命不仅仅是给学生传授应试知识和技巧，更应该提升学生的思维能力和眼界。让学生能带着使命感去学习，培养荣誉感，也是教学活动中不可或缺的一部分。随着国家经济科技的不断进步，对知识生产者的要求会越来越高。国际部，作为一个对外的窗口，应当主动担负起结合中西教育精髓的使命，为祖国未来的教育路线探明方向，为祖国培养更多的知识生产型人才。

科技创新在当今趋于白热化的国际竞争中显得越发重要。小到普通人的生活，大到一个国家的复兴，都和科技的发展密不可分。发现和培养高端科研创新人才，是我们教育者义不容辞的责任，而为了实现高端技术的创新，数学素养的培养是不可或缺的。在中学阶段发现人才并对其进行个性化的定制培养是较为高效的人才培养通道。针对数学能力突出的学生，可以配备一流师资进行个性化培养，在中学阶段树立科技报国梦想，培养基本的科研能力，甚至得到一些有价值的科研成果，从而扎实培养他们未来的科技创新能力。为了给数学能力优秀的同学提供这样一个平台，我们将建立一套以数学和计算机知识为主导的科研培训计划（未来科学家计划），完成该计划的同学，有可能靠自己的能力做出一些原创性的研究并发表会议论文，这样也有更多的机会冲击世界顶级名校。

本课程以简单的多变量微积分在国际上的应用为突破口，让学生接触前沿的数学知识，有助于拓宽其国际视野，明白高等数学可以解决很多实际问题，增加学习的兴趣和信心。

二、课程简介

本课程体系由五次课程组成，每次课程均有明确的主题和目标，课程总结如下表所示。

课程题目以及课程简介

课程题目	课程简介
多元函数入门以及发散思维训练	以最简单的多元函数为例，简述从一元函数到多元函数的思想进程，鼓励学生发散思考，再通过实际应用（等高线、VR 应用），结合教师编写的数学程序让学生加深对原函数的理解，形成一定的研究思考方式
线性代数应用简介以及意识形态	线性代数作为目前通用的基础科研数学方法正在受到越来越多的关注。目前人类的很多科研结果背后都涉及高等代数的运用，因此很有必要在高中阶段介绍一些线性代数的原理而不是简单的运算规则。本章节以诺贝尔奖的科研成果以及芯片设计为起点，详细介绍了高等代数在目前人类科技方面的应用
线性代数理论入门以及中日思维对比	本次课程介绍了高等代数的基础理论，同时阐述了中西方价值观的不同

续表

课程题目	课程简介
自然常数的由来以及金融陷阱判断	结合双十一蚂蚁金服上市遭拒这一热点事件,详细介绍自然常数 e 和指数函数的由来,培养知识生产的意识,同时规避一些简单的金融陷阱,认清资本的本质
中西教育对比以及我们为什么而读书	详细对比中国通才教育和西方精英教育的优缺点,结合大学课本内容、习题安排、思维框架、教学目的等进行系统的对比

三、课程结构

当学生学习完以上课程,可以选择更系统、更专业的科研课程进行学习。该系统学习课程的框架如下。

如果是 9 年级升 10 年级的同学,我们会按照未来科学家计划 1 来进行。首先在 10 年级学习 AP Calculus BC 并拿下 5 分,接着系统地学习以 Java 为主的 AP Computer Science,同时利用俱乐部的时间学习掌握 Python 语言。在 11 年级开学时确定科研项目(项目列表),并且在上半学期和下半学期分别进行多变量微积分以及数学物理方程的学习。

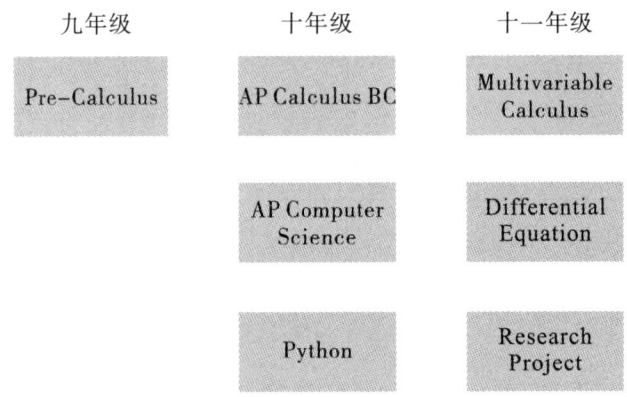

如果是 8 年级升 9 年级的同学,我们的计划分为 3 步。

(1)首先在 9 年级的前一个月学习 AP 微积分在初中阶段没有完成的课程内容,主要是对数和指数函数。之后立即开始 AP Calculus 的学习,并在 9 年级结束时拿下 5 分。

(2)在 10 年级的上下两个学期分别完成 Multivariable Calculus 以及

Differential Equation。至此，完成上述课程的同学，其数学水平将能达到优秀的理工科大学本科二年级学生的水平。

（3）11年级将开始整个计划难度最大同时也是最有价值的部分，在课程开始前，我们会帮助每一位同学选定一个科研方向，然后在接下来的数值计算课程中，我们会从基础的插值（Interpolation）、外推（Extrapolation）等方法开始，然后根据每一位同学选定的科研方向，个性化地带领学生探索有限差分（Finite Difference）、有限元（Finite Element）等数值计算方法。在打开了数值计算的大门后，同学们将有能力对很多问题进行定量分析，比如，预测地震中断层的滑动方向和距离，优化飞行器的外形，解决经济学中的动态模型培养模式，金融市场的资本资产定价模型分析等涉及人类社会生活以及科研活动方方面面的研究课题。这个时候，指导教师和学生之间的关系就会从师生变成合作者，一起来探索某一个未知的问题。同时，我们还将会把优秀的科研成果积极投稿到各行业会议论文。

四、课程实例展示

每一节课都有四个目标：①讲解前沿数学知识；②该前沿知识点的具体应用；③我们为什么要学习这个知识点，这对我们个人和国家会起到什么样的作用；④目前该知识在国内以及国际上的应用。

> The following equations are satisfied:
>
> | Production of | Total output | = | Internal consumption | + | External Demand |
> |---|---|---|---|---|---|
> | farming industry (in tons): | x | = | $0.05x + 0.5y$ | + | 8000 |
> | horse industry: (in 1000km horse rides) | y | = | $0.01x$ | + | 2000 |
>
> In general, let $x_1, x_2, \ldots, x_n$, be the total output of industry $S_1, S_2, \ldots, S_n$, respectively. Then
>
> $$\begin{cases} x_1 = a_{11}x_1 + a_{12}x_1 + \cdots + a_{1n}x_1 + b_1 \\ x_2 = a_{21}x_1 + a_{22}x_1 + \cdots + a_{2n}x_2 + b_2 \\ \cdots \\ x_n = a_{n1}x_1 + a_{n2}x_1 + \cdots + a_{nn}x_n + b_n \end{cases}$$
>
> since $a_{ij}x_j$ is the number of units produced by industry S_i and consumed by industry S_j. The total consumption equals the total production for the product of each industry S_i.
>
> Let
>
> $$A = \begin{pmatrix} a_{11} & \cdots & a_{1n} \\ \vdots & & \vdots \\ a_{n1} & \cdots & a_{nn} \end{pmatrix}, \quad B = \begin{pmatrix} b_1 \\ \vdots \\ b_n \end{pmatrix}, \quad X = \begin{pmatrix} x_1 \\ \vdots \\ x_n \end{pmatrix}$$
>
> A is called the input-output matrix, B the external demand vector and X the production level vector. The above system of linear equations is equivalent to the matrix equation
>
> $$X = AX + B.$$
>
> In the **open Leontief model**, A and $B \neq \begin{pmatrix} 0 \\ \vdots \\ 0 \end{pmatrix}$ are given and the problem is to determine X from this matrix equation.
>
> We can transform this equation as follows:
>
> $$\begin{aligned} I_n X - AX &= B \\ (I_n - A)X &= B \\ X &= (I_n - A)^{-1}B \end{aligned}$$
>
> if the inverse of the matrix $I_n - A$ exists. ($(I_n - A)^{-1}$ is then called the Leontief inverse.) For a given realistic economy, a solution obviously must exist.
>
> For our example we have:
>
> $$A = \begin{pmatrix} 0.05 & 0.5 \\ 0.1 & 0 \end{pmatrix}, \quad B = \begin{pmatrix} 8,000 \\ 2,000 \end{pmatrix}, \quad X = \begin{pmatrix} x \\ y \end{pmatrix}$$

首先，教师基于美方课本讲解数学知识，参考文献有《矢量微积分》(Vector Calculus)、《线性代数及其应用》(Linear Algebra and Its Application)、《微分方程》(Differential Equation)、《计算与数值分析》(Computational and Numerical Analysis)等。学生在学习知识的过程中逐渐掌握知识的来源，有助于他们思考知识的本质，在会基础应用的同时也能够独立完成知识创造，具备初步的科研思维能力。

VR 空間中の旋回移動のための
気流提示手法に関する研究

A Study of Airflow Presentation Method for Turning Motion in Virtual Reality Environment

鈴木勇仁[1], ヤェム ヴィボル[1], 広田光一[2], 雨宮智浩[3], 北崎充晃[4], 池井 寧[1]

Yujin SUZUKI, Vibol YEM, Koichi HIROTA, Tomohiro AMEMIYA, Michiteru KITAZAKI, and Yasushi IKEI

1) 首都大学東京大学院 〒191-0065 東京都日野市旭が丘 6-6, {suzuki,yem,ikei}@vr.sd.tmu.ac.jp
2) 電気通信大学 〒182-8585 東京都調布市調布ヶ丘 1-5-1, hirota@vogue.is.uec.ac.jp
3) 東京大学大学院 〒113-8654 東京都文京区本郷 7 丁目 3-1, amemiya@vr.u-tokyo.ac.jp
4) 豊橋技術科学大学 〒441-8580 愛知県豊橋市天伯町雲雀ヶ丘 1-1, mich@tut.jp

概要：本論文では，旋回移動を伴う視覚刺激に対して，45°刻みの方向からの気流による皮膚感覚刺激を提示した際のバーチャルリアリティ（VR）酔い，ベクションおよび，旋回感覚について調査した結果を述べている．気流の方向に関わらず VR 酔いは軽減され，特に旋回方向と同方向の 45°からの気流提示には，ベクションおよび，旋回感覚を増強させることが示唆された．また，気流提示方向の角度が大きくなるに連れて，進行方向の角度も同様に大きくなっていく傾向があることが示唆された．

キーワード：気流提示，VR 酔い，ベクション，旋回感覚

1. はじめに

視聴覚の情報に関しては，高精細で臨場感の高い再現技術が確立しているが，触覚の情報は提示技術が継続的に開発されている．気流は空間に特有の価値を与える五感情報のひとつである．気流を体験空間に有効に配置するためには，気流の場を任意の空間位置に提示することが必要となる．

本研究は，空間体験の基礎となる歩行に伴う気流の皮膚感覚の知覚特性を調査し制御することにより，身体的追体験の臨場感を高めるとともに VR 酔いを軽減させることを目的としている．

現在，乗馬型運動マシンに乗った状態で，前方から強い風を当てることで，皮膚感覚性の前進ベクションが得られることが報告されている．[1] また，気流による皮膚感覚刺激を与えることで，鳥のような飛行感覚が得られることが報告されている．[2]

本稿では，気流ディスプレイ 5 つと Head Mounted Display（HMD，HTC VIVE PRO）を用いて，VR 空間での旋回移動における気流による VR 酔いの軽減，ベクション及び旋回方向の変化の検証を行った結果を述べる．

2. 気流ディスプレイ

本実験で用いた気流ディスプレイは，気流を生成するサーキュレータ（KL-D992W, Twinbird）のブレード（直径

図 1 気流ディスプレイ（左）と実験風景（左）

16cm），整流グリル，速度制御ドライバ（BXSD120-A, Oriental Motor）から構成され，最大気流速度は正面 0.6m の距離で約 7.0m/s である．

3. 旋回移動における気流提示が与える効果
3.1 目的と手法

旋回移動をするためには HMD 上に示す VR 空間は，視覚的フィードバックとして回転させる必要がある．このような視覚提示は，容易に VR 酔いを引き起こす．この実験の目的は，VR 空間の旋回歩行時における最適（酔いを低減

其次，针对该前沿知识的应用，笔者会结合本人的博士研究经历，搜索相关论文并进行筛选，选择学生感兴趣且难度不大的论文进行分析讲解。例如，在多元函数入门的课程中，笔者介绍了方向导数的知识，在这节课中引用了东京大学关于减轻 VR 的研究论文，该论文指出，通过求解人体转动的方向导数，可以反向制造一个对应的风力场，达到更加拟真和减轻 VR 眩晕感的目的。在高等代数的讲解中，笔者还引出了诺贝尔奖获得者的论文，让学生知道数学知识的应用面是非常广的。

五、课程亮点

```
{{theta, Pi/4, "θ"}, 0, 2Pi, None},
{{t0, 0, Subscript["t", 0]}, -3, 3, None},
{{showplane, True, "show plane"}, {True, False}, ControlPlacement -> Left},
{{showderiv, False, "show tangent"}, {True, False}, ControlPlacement -> Left},
Delimiter,
{{setxy, False, Row[{"set (", Subscript["x", 0], ", ", Subscript["y", 0], ")"}]}, {True, False}, ControlPlacement -> Left},
Delimiter,
{{showsurf, True, "show surface"}, {True, False}, ControlPlacement -> Left},
{{x0, 0}, ControlType -> None},
{{y0, 0}, ControlType -> None},
Initialization :> (rndif[x_] := If[Accuracy[x] == Infinity, x, Round[x, 0.001]];
{{xmin, xmax}, {ymin, ymax}} = {{-3, 3}, {-3, 3}};),
AutorunSequencing -> {1, 2, 3, 4, 7}, TrackedSymbols -> Manipulate
]
```

在课程的制作过程中,教师需要考虑课程难度的问题,其中一些章节是给研究生上课的内容,这部分内容对高中生来讲可能比较困难。在第一节课讲多元函数的过程中,确实出现了一些同学听不懂的情况,尤其是在用全英文授课的前提之下,有不适应感是很正常的,在后续的课程中,笔者先降低了英文授课的比例,然后再慢慢提高英文授课的比例,同时降低对高深知识的讲解,多选取一些有趣的应用，让学生渐渐理解知识的产生过程，从而达到课程设计的目的。

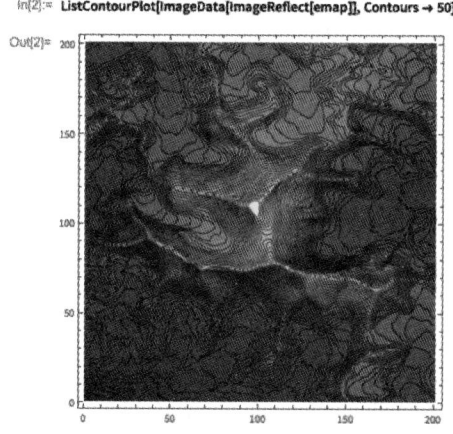

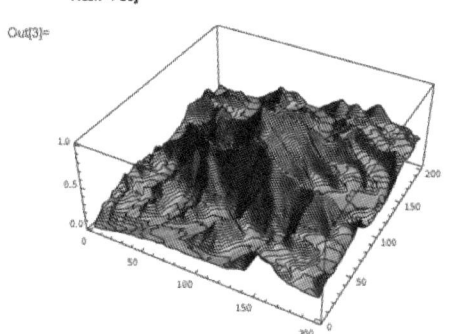

六、课程反思

首先，在培养学生创新精神方面，本课程体系通过打造完整的针对科研的数学基础知识体系，让受教育者构建起完备、系统的科研知识，对知识输出型能力的培养起到了至关重要的作用。其次，本课程体系将中外教育的优势进行了有机的结合，让受教育者对各体系都有更深的认知，同时引入大量的中外科研成果案例，尤其是我国目前的增量成果，以此加强科研报国热情，提升民族自豪感。再次，本套体系能够在高中阶段就让受教育者在解决问题的教学中获得知识和成就感，有助于学生投入到科研的工作中，从而提升我国整体的竞争优势。最后，本文通过分析普高素质课程的教学与反馈，站在授课教师的角度，总结了课程设计，细化了课程目标。通过分析学生的反馈来评价课程体系的优劣，为后续的课程推进以及未来教师的教学活动提供了经验基础。

沟通思想篇

课案九

文化身份认知

课程设计教师：
孙伊然
树德中学国际部托福/雅思/ACT教师
对外经济贸易大学翻译硕士
英语专业八级
曾多次担任国际会议翻译

内容：
一、课程背景
二、教学设计
三、课程教学
四、课堂活动
五、课程反思

一、课程背景

1. 什么是文化身份认知

文化身份认知（Cultural Identity）指一个个体对一种特定文化形成特有文化归属感的过程。这个过程包括学习和接受这种文化的传统、起源、语言、宗教、习俗、思维方式和社会结构。

2. 文化身份认知和文化身份认知危机

15世纪到17世纪，世界地理大发现开启了人类全球化的历程。近一个世纪以来，随着经济和科技的不断发展，不同地区、不同国家之间在经济、政治、文化等方面的联系和依赖空前加强，也促成了人类历史上"大迁徙"。在这样的背景下，很多人尤其是年轻人，会发现自己处于文化身份认知的夹缝中，产生文化身份认知危机（Cultural Identity Crisis）。他们可能是跨文化跨种族家庭的孩子，可能是来自移民家庭的孩子，也有可能是国际学生和难民。这些年轻人，他们有可能从小就面临不同的文化冲突，也有可能在成长的过程中暴露在全新的文化中，开始对自己已有的文化身份认知产生怀疑，再以此为基础构造新的价值观和人生观。

二、教学设计

1. 教学背景分析

（1）目标学生群体：高二学生，学生整体英语水平良好。

（2）教学内容：通过引入学生自身的文化身份认知，探索不同文化对文化中个人的行为和思维所产生的影响，进而以移民为载体探讨多重文化身份（Multicultural Identity）背景下，个人在文化认同以及自我身份认知层面上可能产生的认知冲突。

（3）教学状况及对策分析。

①全英文授课：本次课程为全英文授课，对学生的英语水平有一定程度的要求。同时，教师会以深入浅出的语言解释可能涉及的专有名词以及复杂词汇，也会发放单词表以帮助学生理解一些较为生僻的词汇。

②多次小组讨论：本次课程涉及多次小组讨论环节，教师需要注意小组讨论活动的有效性和对时间的把控。教师在将学生分组后统一发放小组角色卡，

明确小组中每一位成员的角色定位,从而确保小组讨论的顺利进行。

③视频分析引导:本次课程涉及对两段电影电视片段的分析。在毫无头绪的情况下,学生很难对影片片段中隐含的文化内核有深入的理解。为了让学生更好地理解视频内容,教师以电影分析方法为依托,设计了一张视频分析表格,一步步引导学生理解影片中展现的文化冲突。

2. 教学目标设计

本次课程围绕"提升学生全球竞争力"这一国际理解教育的育人目标展开。"提升学生全球竞争力"包含"探索世界""认知多元视角""交流思想"和"展开行动"四个层面。本次课程主要围绕"探索世界""认知多元视角"两个主题展开。通过探索不同文化,甚至多重文化对个体的影响,学生将认识到除了自身文化外的多种文化是如何影响和改变世界的。探讨多重文化身份背景下的个人在文化认同以及自我身份认知层面上可能产生的认知冲突,也将帮助学生从多元的角度发现世界、认识世界。与此同时,课堂上的多次小组活动也锻炼了学生"交流思想"的能力。

三、课程教学

(1) 引入——介绍文化身份认知并进行小组讨论:文化身份认知是如何影响我们的思维方式和行为模式的?

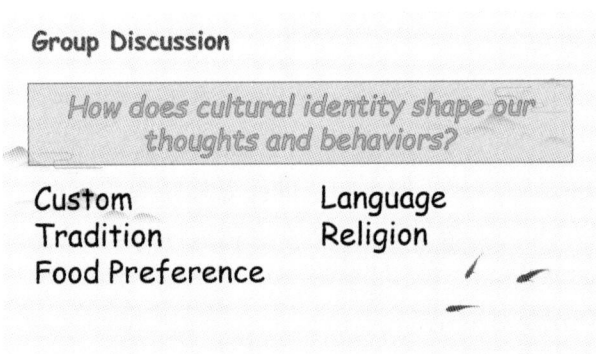

(2) 在小组讨论的基础上,举例东西方文化差异所造成的思维模式和行为模式的不同。

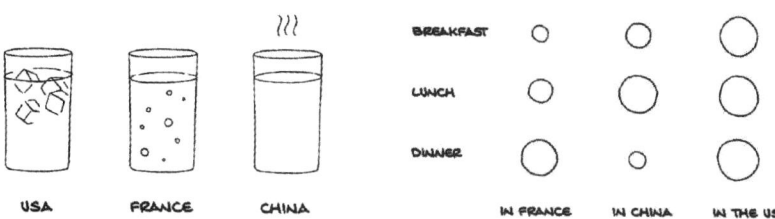

多数情况下,我们自身的文化对我们来说是"隐形"的,但它却能够影响我们对整个世界的认知和看法。只有当我们了解与我们自身的文化所不同的文化时,我们才能够意识到我们的文化身份认知是如何影响我们的认知模式和思维方式的。这个环节可以帮助同学们更直观地认识自己的文化身份认知和其他的文化身份认知在思维模式和行为方式上可能产生的不同甚至冲突。

(3) 影视片段分析——电影《喜福会》和电视剧《初来乍到》影视片段的对比分析。

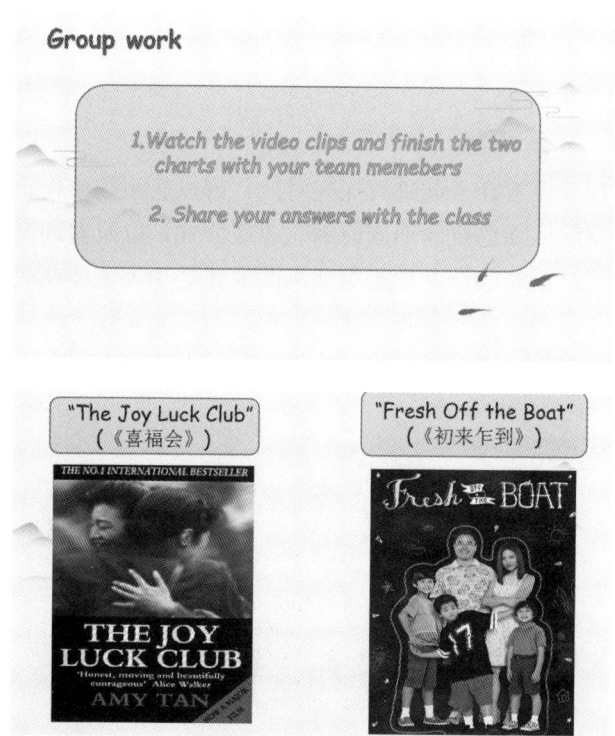

电影《喜福会》改编自美国著名华裔作家谭恩美(Amy Tan)的自传体

沟通思想篇 103

小说，此片从作者的视角讲述了从中国移居美国的四位女性的生活以及她们与美国出生的孩子之间的心理隔阂、感情冲突和文化冲突。电视剧《初来乍到》以 20 世纪 90 年代的美国为背景，从一个孩子的视角讲述了一个华裔家庭在美国奥兰多的创业故事，这个家庭一起憧憬着"美国梦"，与此同时，他们还要竭力保持自己独特的民族文化身份认同。

Chart 1:

	American Influence	Chinese Tradition
Amy Tan		
Eddie		

Chart 2:

	The major characters and their functions	The theme of the scene	The major conflicts	The Climax	The Cultural Dilemma of the leading role (Eddie & Tan)
Clip 1 (Tan)					
Clip 2 (Eddie)					

影视片段对比分析表格

将两个影视片段放在一起进行探究对比，可以从不同年代、不同人的视角分析移民文化身份认知危机的形成原因、表现方式，以及对冲突主体和周遭人事所造成的影响，也能够帮助学生更加全面地体会冲突主体在成长过程中所经历的自我怀疑、自我塑造和自我重建的过程。

（4）诗歌赏析。

Group work

Read the poem "colors" and discuss the following two questions with your teammates.

1. Do you think the writer can ever become truly green?

2. Is it just people with multiple cultural identities who have difficulties finding a place in modern society or are we all restricted by the constraints of society around us? How difficult is it to be an individual at school and outside?

```
Colors (A TCK metaphor)
by Whitni Thomas, MK (1991)

I grew up in a Yellow country        But deep down inside me
But my parents are Blue.             something's Yellow
I'm Blue.                            I love the Blue country.
Or at least, that is what they told me.  But my ways are tinted with Yellow.

But I play with the Yellows.
I went to school with the Yellows.   When I am in the Blue land,
I spoke the Yellow language.         I want to be Yellow.
I even dressed and appeared to be    When I am in the Yellow land,
Yellow.                              I want to be Blue.

Then I moved to the Blue land.       Why can't I be both?
Now I go to school with the Blues.   A place where I can be me.
I speak the Blue language.           A place where I can be green.
I even dress and look Blue.          I just want to be green.
```

在惠特尼·托马斯（Whitni Thomas）的诗"Colors"中，作者从一个孩子的角度出发，使用隐喻的写作手法，讲述了她所遇到的文化身份认同障碍。在诗中，她将自己的原生文化称为"蓝色"，将她所需要融入的新的文化称为"黄色"，她不知道自己是"黄色"的还是"蓝色"的，而她真正想成为的其实是"蓝色"和"黄色"混合的"绿色"。在课堂中，同学们在阅读诗歌之后，会就作者的文化身份认知进行讨论：讨论以作者为代表的，需要融入不同文化语境中的年轻人在进行自我认知的时候可能面临的障碍。接下来，第二个问题帮助同学们跳出文化语境，在更加广阔的社会语境下进行思考：在现代社会中，人们的自我认知是否也会和周围的环境产生冲突，进而影响人们对自我价值的判断？

四、课堂活动

（1）小组讨论。

小组讨论（Group Discussion）是本课程的重要组成部分。小组讨论不仅可以帮助同学们积极地参与到对课堂内容的讨论中，增加学生的参与度，还可以增强课堂的多元性，帮助学生更好地沟通。在此过程中，学生的沟通能力、领导技能、思维能力、分析能力和团队合作精神都得到了锻炼。

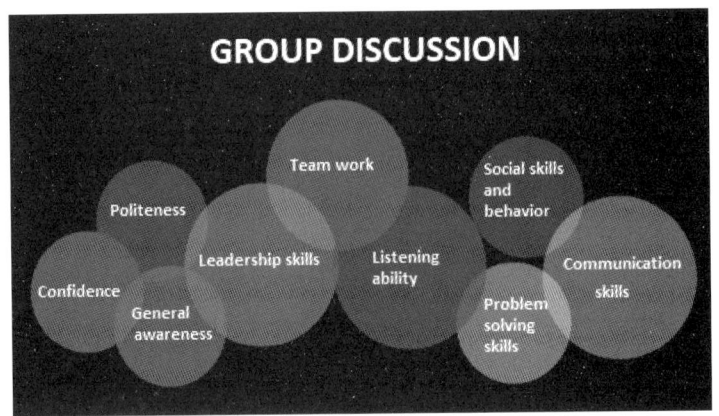

在课堂活动中，六名学生一组，抽签之后每一个学生会获得一个角色，学生在本堂课的小组活动中需要扮演好自己的角色，在组长（The Chair）的领导下，完成课程中展开的一系列小组活动。

Group Work Roles

The chair
Make sure the team achieves its tasks

The resource manager
Call the teacher over if your team has a group question
Organize your team's clean-up efforts

The scribe
Record the team's discussion

The facilitator
Make sure everybody in the group has equal chance to contribute

The time keeper
Make sure the group keeps to time

The presenter
Present your team's result to the class

（2）影视作品分析。

丰富的影视素材可以让学生接触到社会和文化的许多方面。影视作品分析可以帮助同学们直观生动地了解中西方文化的冲突和主角的内在冲突，并能透过表层文化了解影视作品背后的价值观念和思维方式。

比如，在同学们对《初来乍到》这一影视素材进行分析时，他们会先看到主角，一个华裔小男孩 Eddie Huang 和当地的白人小孩因为喜欢同一名歌手而迅速打成一片，当他们正热火朝天地讨论这位歌手的新专辑时，Eddie 从包里拿出他的午饭——一盒面条。而那位前一秒还对他很友善的白人同学迅速露出了嫌弃的眼神，并要求 Eddie 离开餐桌。这一具有戏剧效果的反转一开始让同学们哄堂大笑，但当他们看到 Eddie 回家后不愿意吃妈妈做的面条并要求妈妈带他到当地超市买和白人同学一样的食物时，同学们陷入了思考。

影视片段从一件学生餐厅的小事展开，生动地呈现出亚裔群体在融入当地社会的过程中可能面临的文化冲突，也通过 Eddie Huang 的视角表现了在双重文化夹缝中的孩子所必须面临的文化选择。影视分析往往能够使同学们有更加强烈的代入感，帮助他们更直观地理解课堂主题。而作为辅助手段的影视分析表格，则可以让同学们在观看影片的同时提取出与课堂主题相关的重要信息，理解影片和课程内容之间的关联。

（3）诗歌赏析。

本次课程以英文诗歌赏析作为结尾，从诗歌出发，展现课程立意，从文化语境过渡到社会语境，从文化身份认同过渡到自我身份认同。

诗歌是人类情感的最高级载体之一，在诗歌中，作者往往能够通过各类修辞方式和韵律自由地表达情感，而读者也能从诗歌中获得深深的情感共鸣。本课中选取的诗歌"Colors"与课程主题完全呼应，作者通过暗喻、意象、排比等一系列修辞手法，将诗歌情感推向高潮。而最后的开放性问题又进一步地将学生产生的情感共鸣带入他们的现实生活中，这有助于更好地训练学生的批判性思维能力，同时帮助学生更深入地理解本门课程的现实意义。

五、课程反思

中国青少年，作为祖国未来的栋梁和希望，应该保持开放的心态，拥抱世界，探索世界。当今世界，各种文化观念和社会意识形态的冲突加剧，本次课程旨在引导青少年在面对他国文化冲击时保持辩证思考的能力、清醒的文化认知和自我认知，帮助他们成为拥有中国情怀和世界眼光的新一代世界公民。

课案十

新加坡英语

课程设计教师：

孙伊然

树德中学国际部托福/雅思/ACT教师

对外经济贸易大学翻译硕士

英语专业八级

曾多次担任国际会议翻译

内容：

一、课程背景

二、课程设置

三、课堂活动

四、课程反思

一、课程背景

本次课程是前一个单元"Cultural Identity"（文化身份认同）的一个延展性课程。"Cultural Identity"（文化身份认同）着眼于亚裔群体在中西文化背景下所产生的文化身份探索。而本次课程则是在认知他人、认知自我、产生沟通的交汇点上探讨融合文化下的文化碰撞和可能产生的独特语言现象，而这一语言现象又反过来影响文化和身份认同本身。

之所以会选择新加坡英语作为课程的主题，是因为新加坡具有特殊的历史和语言的独特性。新加坡作为一个拥有复杂殖民历史的国家，受西方文化、马来文化、印度文化等多种文化的影响。而新加坡华人众多，这些文化与主流的中国文化相融合，形成了独特的文化氛围和特殊的英语方言。这种独特的文化身份认知是许多代华人华侨探索而来的。本着"人类命运共同体"的价值导向原则，秉承着比较研究的研究方法，以提升国际竞争力为核心，学习新加坡的独特历史文化以及承载这种文化的特殊语言，可以给同学们提供一个全新的角度来增强自己中华民族的身份认同，让同学们认识到坚实的文化身份认同对一个人的重要性，对一个民族、一个国家的重要性。同时，本着探究思辨的原则，本课程深入讨论语言与文化之间的关系，以及不同的语言在文化沟通中所起到的作用。

二、课程设置

（1）引入：小组讨论——语言是否和你的文化传统息息相关。

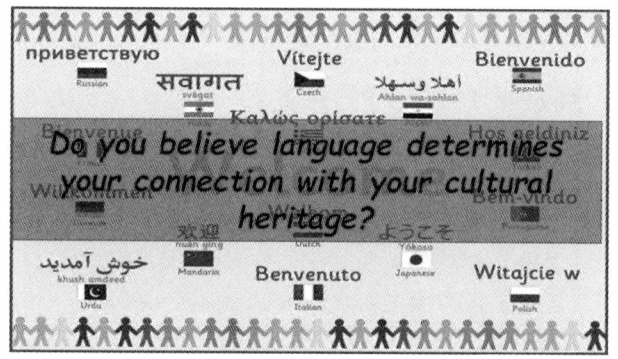

（2）背景介绍——新加坡历史以及新加坡英语的由来。

早期英国殖民者于19世纪来到新加坡，并在当地兴办学校，新加坡英语便起源于英办学校中。最早的新加坡英语很可能是一种洋泾浜语（Pidgin），是不会说英语的人在街头说的一种混合语。其语法简单，发音不稳定，非英语成分很大，受到印度英语、马来语、汉语等多方面的影响。随着时间的推移，早期的洋泾浜语在新加坡社会各个层面推广，并由新一代的新加坡人以母语的形式学习，语音、语法、词汇等逐渐定性，日趋成熟，成为一种完全成熟的英语方言。

（3）介绍新加坡英语的独特规则，学习一些常见的新加坡英语用法。通过小组活动和课堂展示引导学生学习新加坡英语。

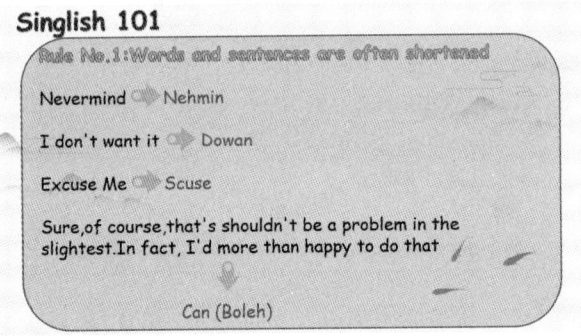

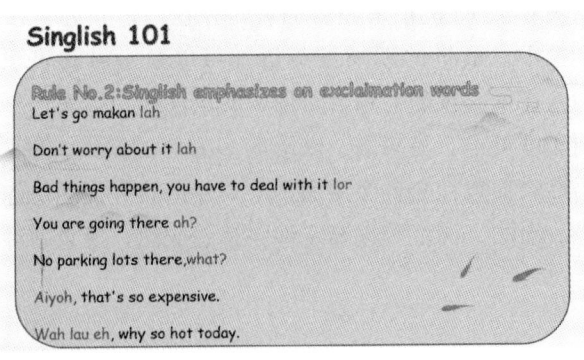

（4）阅读文章——《新加坡英语：不地道的英语还是独特身份的勋章？》（"SINGLISH：Broken English or Badge of Identity？"）并讨论与文章主题相关的问题。

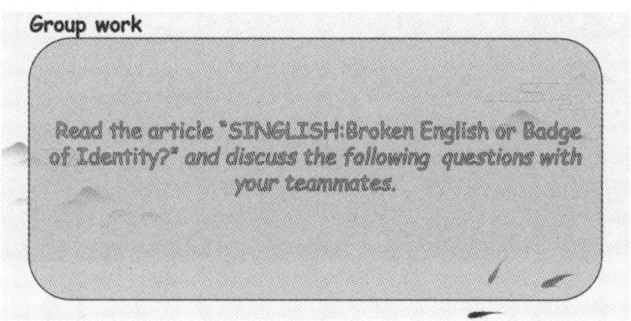

（5）小组讨论——语言对文化的影响以及新加坡如何通过独特的语言寻求整个民族的文化身份定位。

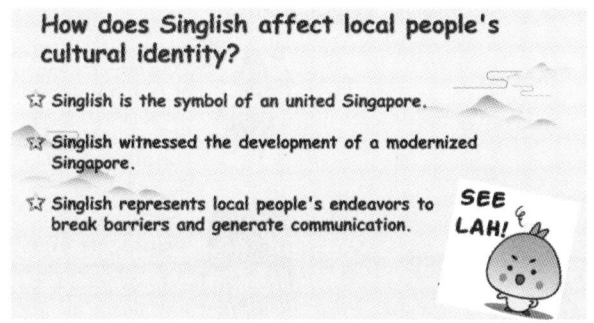

三、课堂活动

（1）小组讨论。

小组讨论（Group Discussion）是本课的一个重要组成部分。小组讨论不仅可以帮助同学们积极地参与到对课堂内容的讨论中，增加学生的参与度，还可以增强课堂的多元性，帮助学生更好地沟通。在此过程中，学生的沟通能力、领导技能、思维能力、分析能力和团队合作精神都得到了锻炼。

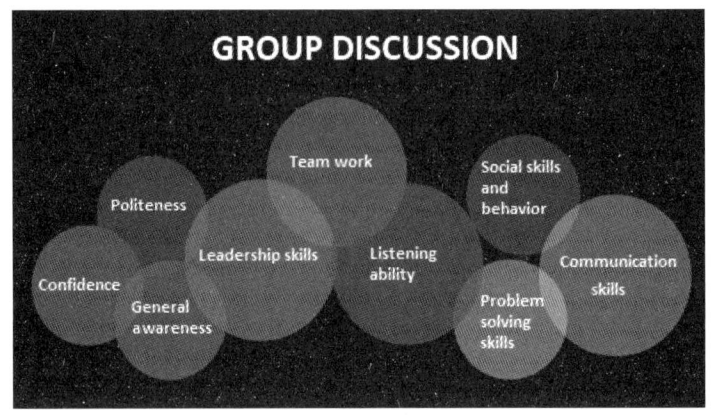

在课堂活动中,六名学生一组,抽签之后每一个学生都会获得一个角色,学生在本堂课的小组活动中需要扮演好自己的角色,在组长(The Chair)的领导下,完成课程中的一系列小组活动。

Group Work Roles

 The chair Make sure the team achieves its tasks

 **The resource manager** Call the teacher over if your team has a group question Organize your team's clean-up efforts

 The scribe Record the team's discussion

 **The facilitator** Make sure everybody in the group has equal chance to contribute

 **The time keeper** Make sure the group keeps to time

 **The presenter** Present your team's result to the class

(2)视频分析。

多媒体教学形象生动,能够增大课堂教学容量,由于多媒体能向学生提供声、像、图、文等综合信息,更有利于吸引学生的注意力,激发学生的学习兴趣,提高学生在学习中的主观能动性。

在本次课堂中,笔者引入了对比新加坡英语和标准英语的视频,视频能有效提高课堂的趣味性,让抽象的课堂具象化。学生可以通过视频中两位主播生动的表演,直观地感受新加坡英语和标准英语在语言构成上的区别,并认识到这种特殊方言形成的文化背景。

（3）新加坡英语模仿秀。

"一起来说新加坡英语吧！"这是本堂课最有意思，也是同学们参与度特别高的一个环节。同学们平时被要求一本正经地说英语，还不停地被纠正语音语调，这次终于可以放松地说一次英语了。

新加坡英语模仿秀这个环节可以将同学们立刻带入新加坡快节奏的、随性的、交融的文化氛围中。相比语法规则，新加坡英语更加注重交流的语言特性，这也带给它随性轻松，仿佛一切难题都能迎刃而解的轻快语调。

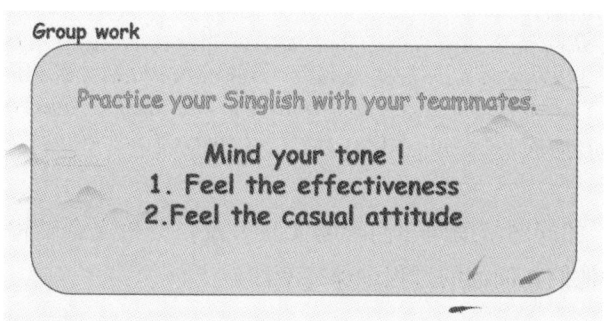

Practice your Singlish !

English	Singlish
Where shall we eat?	Where you want to makan?
It is going to rain soon.	Going to rain already lah.
Why did you take such a long time to eat?	Why take so long to eat, ah?
Do you serve coffee?	You got kopi?
My goodness! He's really late!	Wah lau eh! So late!
Are you sure they have it here?	Here have, meh?
You can't sit over there.	There can sit lah.
You can take this first.	You bring go first.
I have no choice but to go down town.	No choice, must go downtown lor.
Can you reserve this table?	For me chope this table, meh?

（4）文章阅读策略。

本次课程的阅读活动在"阅读前""阅读中""阅读后"均设置了问题环节。

沟通思想篇

"阅读前"的问题帮助同学们明确阅读的目标。

> *Before Reading Questions*:
> →*Before you read her blog, imagine you were living in another country and make a list of the aspects of society you might comment on. In what order of importance might you put the different topics? Why would you give certain aspects more importance than others?*
> →*There are many different varieties of English throughout the world. Who decides what is good English or bad English?* →*What is the difference between an accent and a dialect?*
> →*Think about your own culture and society. Are there many different accents and dialects? Which ones have high status or prestige and which do not? Why?*
> →*Do you use the same accent and dialect at all times or does your language change depending on the social context you find yourself in? Why is this?*

"阅读中"的问题帮助同学们理解文章大意,分析文章结构,熟悉生词和句型,也帮助他们在阅读的过程中保持专注。

> *During Reading Questions*:
> *From the list below, choose an appropriate heading for paragraphs 1-8.*
> *There are more headings than you will need.*
> *A In print*
> *B The future of Singlish*
> *C A national badge*
> *D First impressions*
> *E Grammatical features*
> *F Local culture*
> *G Origins*
> *H Singapore accents*
> *I Singlish in the local media*
> *J Pronunciation*
> *K Language flexibility*
> *L The official view*
> *Find synonyms for the following words in the text.*
> *a incessant*
> *b painstakingly*
> *c verbalization*
> *d tumultuous*
> *e indigenous*
> *f laconic*

"阅读后"的问题帮助学生总结、讨论、反思文章的主题。

> *After reading questions*：
> 1. *According to the writer, why did Singlish develop? How did Singlish develop?*
> 2. *What were the two features of spoken Singlish that the writer noticed?*
> 3. *In what ways is the grammar of written Singlish different to standard English?*
> 4. *Why is there no single variety of Singlish?*
> 5. *Why does the Singapore government criticize the use of Singlish?*
> 6. *How do educated Singaporeans use Singlish?*
> 7. *What is the writer's overall view of Singlish?*
> 8. *Can you combine Singlish with the history and the cultural identity of the Singaporeans?*
> 9. *Think about the ways in which you learned your second language. We can learn grammar intuitively, without conscious thought, or formally, by stating rules. What are the strengths and weaknesses of each approach?*

同时,"阅读后"问题中也设置有一些开放性问题,这些问题可以帮助学生更深入地讨论语言与文化之间的相互影响。

比如:

问题 1 "Can you combine Singlish with the history and the cultural identity of the Singaporeans?"

这个问题可以引导学生思考文化与语言之间的关系。

问题 2 "Do you use the same accent and dialect at all times or does your language change depending on the social context you find yourself in? Why is this?"

这个问题不仅引导学生讨论语言对文化的影响,也引导学生通过自己的亲身体验探讨方言与文化以及语言社会环境之间的关系。

问题 3 "Think about the ways in which you learned your second language. We can learn grammar intuitively, without conscious thought, or formally, by stating rules. What are the strengths and weaknesses of each approach?"

开放性问题能积极帮助学生探索不同的学习方法。通过了解新加坡英语这个特殊的语言变体,同学们可能会对语言学习的方法有不一样的认知。

四、课程反思

在第一节国际理解课程上,笔者曾经问过同学们:什么是国际理解?有一位同学的回答让人印象深刻,他说:"国际理解就是中国文化和西方文化的交流。"这位同学的答案虽然简单,却能够体现国际理解课程的核心——交流思想。

从交流思想这一主题,笔者想到了新冠肺炎疫情下一些国家对中国,甚至对华裔群体的部分过激言论和行为。国际理解,是站在世界的角度看问题,也是站在民族的角度看问题。从民族的角度看问题,不仅要考虑到中国大陆人民,也要考虑到海外的华人华侨。他们是中国文化的早期传播者,也是国际理解和国际交流的先驱,在这个特殊的时期,他们的声音应该被听到,他们诉求也应该被看到。同学们作为国家未来的主人,可以更深入地思考:在国际舞台上,中华民族应如何让国际社会对中国的文化和中国的发展有更加客观和公正的认知。

课案十一

构建包容性的社会

课程设计教师:

魏敏

英国杜伦大学英语教育硕士

曾在剑桥大学跟随知名作家 Derek Niemann 进修一年创意写作

荣获第四届"黑布林英语阅读"全国优课大赛一等奖

荣获四川省教育厅四川师范大学基础教育课程研究中心 2021 英语学科"整本书阅读"说课比赛一等奖

内容:

一、教学对象分析

二、教学内容分析

三、教学目标

四、教学方法

五、教学过程

六、作业布置

七、教学亮点

八、教学反思

一、教学对象分析

本堂课的教学对象是国家级重点高中高二年级学生,高中同学备战高考压力大,大部分时间都用在刷题上,正所谓"两耳不闻窗外事,一心只读圣贤书"。这样下去,学生可能会不自觉地成为北京大学钱理群教授所说的"精致的利己主义者"。"精致的利己主义者"的表现之一便是对社会淡漠,对他人旁观。作为教师,要在高中学生人格形成的关键阶段,有意识地培养学生成为更有温度的人,避免学生在成为"精致的利己主义者"的路上越走越远。

二、教学内容分析

本次的教学内容为构建包容性的社会(An Inclusive Society),根据联合国定义,包容性社会指的是一个超越种族、性别、阶级、代际和地理差异的社会,该社会能确保其中的所有成员有能力且平等地确立一整套大众认可的社会管理机构体制。(英文原文定义:An inclusive society is a society that overrides differences of race, gender, class, generation, and geography, and ensures inclusion, equality of opportunity as well as capability of all members of the society to determine an agreed set of social institutions that govern social interaction. ——Expert Group Meeting on Promoting Social Integration, Helsinki, July 2008)。

当今社会,残障人士很难享有跟其他健康成员一样平等的权益和条件去参与社会活动。联合国数据显示,全球有10亿残障人士,约占总人口的15%。残障问题还与教育、贫困、就业、歧视、暴力等问题紧密相连。本次构建包容性的社会课程从残障主题入手,目的是让学生认识该主题的重要性,了解国内外残障事业的发展,激发学生对困难群体的关爱之情,树立对社会主义核心价值观"平等"的信仰。

本堂课采取全英文教学,教学时长约为2+1节课,共计约120分钟。前两节课讲授新知识,第三节课为作业汇报和点评课。

三、教学目标

1. 知识和能力
（1）识别残障类型。
（2）分析理解残障群体需求。
（3）探究关爱残障人士和困难群体的必要性。
2. 过程与方法
（1）调研需求，设计产品：学生根据残障人士需求，设计无障碍设施。
（2）对比评价各国残障政策差异，思考中国残障政策可以改进的方面。
3. 情感态度和价值观
（1）培养关爱困难群体的慈悲心。
（2）树立对社会主义核心价值观"平等"的信仰。

四、教学方法

教学方法包括情景教学法、案例分析法、小组讨论法、探究式学习法、项目式教学法。

五、教学过程

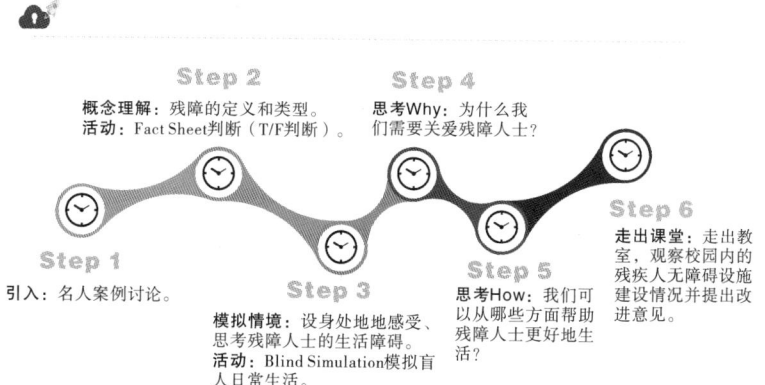

Step 1
引入：名人案例讨论。

Step 2
概念理解：残障的定义和类型。
活动：Fact Sheet判断（T/F判断）。

Step 3
模拟情境：设身处地地感受、思考残障人士的生活障碍。
活动：Blind Simulation模拟盲人日常生活。

Step 4
思考Why：为什么我们需要关爱残障人士？

Step 5
思考How：我们可以从哪些方面帮助残障人士更好地生活？

Step 6
走出课堂：走出教室，观察校园内的残疾人无障碍设施建设情况并提出改进意见。

沟通思想篇

Step 1：导入——人物案例。从知名残疾物理学家霍金引入残障主题。

英国著名残障物理学家霍金

教师面向全班同学提问：
(1) 图片中的人物是谁？
(2) 你知道哪些关于霍金的事迹？霍金得了什么病？对身体有哪些影响？
(3) 霍金不能说话，是什么帮助他说话的呢？如果没有这个语音合成设备，他还能自由地跟这个世界交流吗？我们还能聆听来自霍金的物理理论吗？

在回答第二个问题的时候，没有一个同学会描述霍金的疾病：运动神经元疾病（Motor Neurone Disease）。这时教师告知答案，可以引起同学们对新知识的兴趣。教师紧接着提问：运动神经元疾病会对霍金的身体造成什么影响？学生回答其中的影响之一是不能说话。教师接着提问：是什么帮助霍金说话的呢？学生此时知道该设备的中文名称，但是却不能用英语表达，教师告知学生答案，这个设备叫"Speech-Generating Device"（语音合成设备）。教师接着引导学生思考：如果没有这个语音合成设备，他还能自由地跟这个世界交流吗？我们还能聆听来自霍金的物理理论吗？

教师点题：我们的生活中有非常多像霍金一样的残障人士，如果他们都能像霍金一样获得帮助，那么他们不仅能够更好地独立生活，也许还能给人类社会创造非凡价值。

Step 2：概念导入——师生问答＋教师讲解残障类型。

教师提问：大家知道哪些残障类型呢？同学们分小组讨论1分钟后发言。同学们大多能提到与身体相关的残疾，如运动、视力、听力障碍等，但是心理健康障碍、智力障碍、学习障碍等几乎没人提到。

残障类型的六种分类

教师结合案例对学生不太熟悉的心理健康障碍、智力障碍和学习障碍进行讲解。

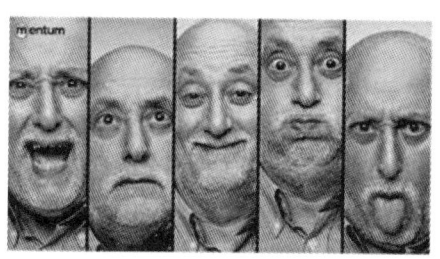

心理健康障碍"躁郁症""多重人格障碍"

沟通思想篇　121

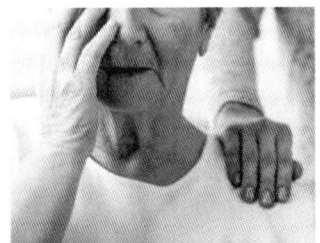

智力障碍"唐氏综合征""阿尔茨海默病"

学习障碍"语言听、说、读、写障碍""多动症"

- How would you feel if you received student's homework like this?

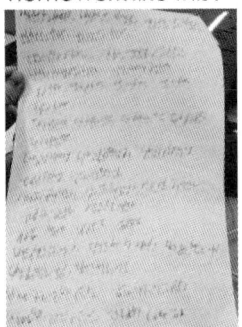
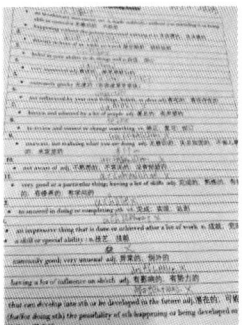

真实案例分析——新学期开始"我"收到的一份"潦草的作业"

这里，有必要单独对上图中的案例进行说明。这是发生在笔者身上的真实案例。在新学期第二周的时候给同学们听写单词，有一位同学的字迹几乎不可辨认，歪歪扭扭，笔者下意识地非常生气，认为这是该同学不认真对待作业的体现。但出于该生是高一新生，笔者还是决定观察一段时间再评价，以免伤害到学生。之后听该生班主任提到，该生有阅读和书写双重障碍，无法像普通人一般正常阅读文字，也无法书写出工整字迹。由此案例，笔者反思到，自己作为教师，对学习障碍的了解几乎是空白的，甚至把学习障碍等同于态度不端，真是无知至极。

课堂活动：在学生对残障主题有了概念性的了解之后，教师给学生发放 True or False Fact Sheet，让学生结合背景知识进行正误判断。此活动旨在纠正同学们对残障议题存在的一些误区，同时拓宽同学们有关残障议题的知识面。

Fact Sheet：学生版

Task：Decide whether each of the following statement is true or false?

Fact sheet on People with Disabilities

Overview

1. Around 15% of the world's population, or estimated 1 billion people, live with disabilities. They are the world's second largest minority.

2. In countries with life expectancies over 70 years, individuals spend on average about 8 years, or 11.5% of their life span, living with disabilities.

3. 50% of persons with disabilities live in developing countries, according to the UN Development Programme.

4. In most OECD countries, women report higher incidents of disability than men.

5. The World Bank estimates that 10% of the world's poorest people have some kind of disability, and tend to be regarded in their own communities as the most disadvantaged.

6. According to UNICEF, 30% of street youths have some kind of disability.

7. Comparative studies on disability legislation shows that only 45 countries have anti-discrimination and other disability-specific laws.

Education

1. 50% of children with disabilities in developing countries do not attend school.

2. The global literacy rate for adults with disabilities is as low as 3%, and 1% for women with disabilities.

Employment

1. An estimated 386 million of the world's working-age people have some kind of disability, says the International Labour Organization (ILO). Unemployment among the persons with disabilities is as high as 80% in some countries. Often employers assume that persons with disabilities are unable to work.

2. Companies report that employees with disabilities have better retention rates, reducing the high cost of turnover. After one year of employment, the retention rate of persons with disabilities is 85%.

3. Thousands of persons with disabilities have been successful as small business owners. Persons with disabilities have a higher rate of self-employment and small business experience (12.2%) than persons without disabilities (7.8%).

Violence

1. In some countries, up to a quarter of disabilities result from injuries and violence, says WHO.

2. Persons with disabilities are more likely to be victims of violence or rape, and less likely to obtain police intervention, legal protection or preventive care.

3. Research indicates that violence against children with disabilities occurs at annual rates at least 1.7 times greater than for their peers without disabilities.

本活动答案可参看联合国 Department of Economic and Social Affairs Disability 的网站：*https://www.un.org/development/desa/disabilities/resources/factsheet-on-persons-with-disabilities.html*

Step 3：模拟情境——设身处地地感受并思考残障人士的生活障碍。

学生在课堂上模拟盲人生活

光有理论知识是不够的，同学们对于残障人士的困难仍然难有共鸣。因此，笔者设计了体验盲人生活的活动，邀请学生带上眼罩，完成如穿衣、开门、找东西、回到座位等任务。学生带上眼罩之后，行动自然会笨拙许多。活动结束后，学生分享了自己的体验和感想。由此，大家被带入到模拟的残障人士生活情境中，更能设身处地地理解残障人士的生活困难。

Step 4：思考为什么我们需要关爱残障人士。

沟通思想篇　125

接下来，为了让同学们从内心理解这个议题的重要性，教师需要带领学生思考探究为什么我们要关注残障议题。在此部分中，学生先小组讨论5分钟，之后小组代表发言陈述，最后教师进行总结。

关注残障议题的原因包括但不限于：①残障人口众多，据联合国数据显示，全球约有10亿残障人士，占据总人口的15%。我国有8500万残障人士。残障问题还与教育、贫困、就业、歧视、暴力等问题紧密相连。②作为发展中国家，我国的残障事业还相对落后，值得关注。③残障人士可能就是我们亲近的朋友家人，甚至我们自己在人生中的某个阶段受了伤，也会碰到和残障人士一样的生活障碍，残障问题不是"他们"的问题，而是"我们"共同的问题。

Step 5：思考我们可以从哪些方面帮助残障人士更好地生活。

要了解如何帮助残障人士，首先要了解残障人士会碰到哪些障碍。在这个部分中，教师引导学生结合生活场景归纳总结残障人士会遇到的障碍类型：一般包含态度、组织和系统、信息沟通、建筑、技术五项障碍。学生阅读补充材料"Understanding Barriers to Accessibility"，详细理解五大障碍的具体表现。

Understanding Barriers to Accessibility

COUNCIL OF ONTARIO UNIVERSITIES
CONSEIL DES UNIVERSITÉS DE L'ONTARIO

What is accessibility?

Accessibility is a general term used to describe the degree to which a product, device, service, or environment is available to be used by all intended audiences. According to the Government of Ontario, there are five identified barriers to accessibility for persons with disabilities. These barriers are attitudinal, organizational or systemic, architectural or physical, information or communications, and technology.

As an educator, you have a responsibility to accommodate students with disabilities under the *Ontario Human Rights Code*. Requests for accommodation are made on an individual basis by students through the Office for Students with Disabilities and require medical and/or formal documentation.

Under the *Accessibility for Ontarians with Disabilities Act*, you also have a responsibility to learn about accessibility for persons with disabilities and how it relates to the development and delivery of accessible programs and courses. To create an accessible learning environment, educators must be aware of the barriers that affect student learning and educational opportunities, and they must proactively remove the barriers that are within their control.

What are the five barriers to accessibility?

1. Attitudinal

Attitudinal barriers are behaviours, perceptions, and assumptions that discriminate against persons with disabilities. These barriers often emerge from a lack of understanding, which can lead people to ignore, to judge, or have misconceptions about a person with a disability.

Examples of attitudinal barriers include:

- Assuming a person with a disability is inferior.

- Assuming that someone with a speech impairment cannot understand you.

- Forming ideas about a person because of stereotypes or a lack of knowledge.

- Making a person feel as though you are doing them a "special favour" by providing their accommodations.

（阅读材料完整文章参见：https://www.uottawa.ca/respect/sites/www.uottawa.ca.respect/files/accessibility-cou-understanding-barriers-2013-06.pdf）

学生可根据不同的障碍类型思考如何建立无障碍设施和相关法规政策。

Step 6：走出课堂——走出教室观察校园内的残疾人无障碍设施建设情况并提出改进意见。

在课堂中抽出 20 分钟时间，让同学们走出教室，走到校园的各个角落，去观察哪里有残障设施。所有小组回来时都说学校里几乎没有残障设施。

案例展示：这时候，教师给学生播放视频，展示世界上在无障碍设施方面建设较好的校园，让学生们感受无障碍校园的生活。然后，教师引导同学们思考：我们的校园可以进行哪些无障碍设施的改造呢？学生进行小组讨论，发挥创意，教师给予点评。最后，教师总结主题。我们要构建一个包容性的社会，就要让在身体或者心理智力处于弱势的群体平等地参与社会活动。残障群体不是"他们"，这个包容性的社会是我们共同的生存空间。

六、作业布置

小组作业——创意设计：根据课堂上分析的残障人士的生活障碍，设计一个可以帮助残疾人更加便利地生活的无障碍设施。学生需要画出简图并撰写简要的英文使用说明。教师要提醒学生进行案例收集，以积累创意素材，同时注意做需求分析，保障设计出来的产品有实用性。

以下作业二选一：

（1）小组作业——校外实地考察：学生周末去公园、博物馆、图书馆等调研无障碍设施建设情况并提出改进意见。

（2）小组作业——政策措施对比研究：学生收集并对比不同国家（至少 4 个国家，含中国）的残障政策措施，并讨论我国在残障政策和措施方面还有哪些可以提升的地方。请用表格呈现主要政策措施的差异，并提出至少三点我国在残障政策措施方面可以改进之处。教师需要在资料检索和对比表格的设计上给予学生一定的指导。

教师需要协调保证两项作业都有一定数量的小组参与。

七、教学亮点

（1）情景模拟：学生模拟盲人生活场景，切身感受盲人生活的不易。

（2）案例选取：本次课程选取了笔者自己的学生（匿名）作为书写障碍的

案例，旨在让同学们认识到与有运动障碍、视觉听觉障碍等的残障人士相比，有智力障碍、学习障碍（如书写障碍、阅读障碍等）、心理健康障碍等的残障人士更容易被大众忽略，导致他们的困难不容易得到解决。

（3）实践设计：走出课堂，去调研自己最直接且接触最多的环境——校园的残障设施建设情况，让同学们将理论与实际联系，进行更深入的学习。

（4）作业设计：课后作业设计均为小组作业，小组作业可以锻炼同学们的协调沟通和合作能力。

八、教学反思

本次课程由于课时有限，笔者对于学生课后作业里的创意设计、校外实地考察、政策措施对比研究等的操作方法的指导不够。在后期教学中，笔者还应该给予高中生更多的教学指导（Scaffolding），让学生带着方法离开课堂，从而有能力进行独立探索，成为知识海洋里的"渔夫"。

课案十二

宽窄巷子研学设计

课程设计教师：
周丹
ETS EAP 认证教师
剑桥 Teaching and Learning 执教资格
GCDF 职业规划师
内容：
一、课程背景和理念
二、课程实施
三、课程反思
四、作业展示

一、课程背景和理念

EAP（English for Academic Purpose，学术英语）是树德中学国际部的校本课程，该课程体系建设在全球胜任力的框架下进行，并由 EAP 文化、EAP 语言、EAP 批判思维组成。该课程的整体框架借鉴了 IB 课程体系，并旨在培养 21 世纪学生的未来核心能力：批判思维能力、研究能力和实践能力。在课程教学上，我们采取了几个课程的联动教学，从语言、文化和思维方面培养学生的全球胜任力。

成都作为西南地区的国际化大都市有着悠久的历史。成都是全国十大古都和首批国家历史文化名城。成都金沙遗址距今已有约3000年历史，周太王以"一年成聚，二年成邑，三年成都"，故名成都；蜀汉、成汉、前蜀、后蜀等政权先后在此建都；汉朝时期成都为全国五大都会之一；到了唐代，成都为中国最发达的工商业城市之一，史称"扬一益二"；北宋时成都是汴京以外第二大都会，出现了世界上最早使用的纸币"交子"。成都还拥有都江堰、武侯祠、杜甫草堂等名胜古迹。

闻名全国的宽窄巷子是成都文化的一颗明珠，是成都少城的重要组成部分。少城，又称满城，位于成都老城区西部，是清朝朝廷为八旗兵及其家属专门修建的"城中城"。平定三藩之乱后，成都地区的八旗兵逐渐增多，于是清政府于1718年在成都城西部修建了满城，由于处在战国时期秦人张仪修建的少城遗址上，故人称"少城"。清朝统治末期，满汉互不往来的规矩逐渐被打破，少城内的八旗子弟早年确由成都将军按照祖制供养，此时已经不能为继，破落的旗人子弟开始偷出城外，想尽一切办法谋生；城外的汉族人由此也可以偷入满城之内，做旗人的生意。双方逐渐融合、通婚，促进了满汉的民族大融合。成都少城区域的变迁也是成都历史文化变迁的一面镜子。

作为国际理解课程，我们希望学生能够通过对少城区域的商业开发的研究，体会到成都的发展，同时反思商业开发是否对文化的传承和保护有益。这次课程采取研究性学习方式，激发学生自主学习能力，培养学生追求卓越的态度，以及发现问题、提出问题、解决问题的能力；以学生从学习生活和社会生活中获得的各种课题或项目设计、作品的设计与制作等为基本的学习载体；以在提出问题和解决问题的全过程中学习到的科学研究方法、获得的丰富且多方面的体验和科学文化知识为基本内容。研究性学习不同于综合课程，虽然在很多情况下，其涉及的知识是综合的，但是它不是几门学科综合而成的课程，也不等同于活动课程。虽然研究性学习是学生开展的自主活动，但它不是一般的活动，而是以科学研究为主的课题研究活动；它也不等同于问题课程，虽然它也以问题为载体，但不是接受性学习，而是以研究性学习为主要学习方式的课程。

二、课程实施

（1）澄清或识别问题。我们在前期让学生阅读了《成都街巷志》，这本书的作者是著名巴蜀文化研究专家袁庭栋，他以20多年的资料积累和4年多的考察与写作，用了70万字和1209幅图片，图文并茂地展示了成都500多条街巷，以及城池、河道、桥梁的命名缘由、历史变迁、街巷中的名人掌故、趣闻轶事，重要的历史事件与民俗活动、重要的学校、企业、地下出土的历史文物。全书资料丰富、论述严谨、文字流畅、引人入胜。书中编有地名索引和珍贵的历史地图，具有实用价值。还有博物馆、图书馆、档案馆的藏品和部分私人收藏。这些丰富翔实的内容能让学生全面认识老成都的历史，尤其是少城区域的历史，让学生了解历史与城市发展的关系。

（2）针对问题提出假设，或者提出解决问题的想法或思路。成都开始老城区改造时，少城地区的宽窄巷子增加了很多餐饮店铺和小资的咖啡厅、冰激凌店、小吃店等。但是商业化的改造是否保留了原有的文化？

（3）围绕问题解决，制订一个初步的研究计划。学生在分组后围绕少城老城区的商业改造，思考什么是文化传承与保留？文化的传承与保留与商业化的关系是什么？商业化的改造是否可以保留原有的文化？

（4）按计划采取行动。学生通过问卷、观察、访谈、查阅文献资料、搜集事物作品等形式，获取解决问题所需要的资料信息。学生在实地调查采访前制订观察和采访计划，并在教师带领下去宽窄巷子进行实地调研。

学生参与实地调研

（5）对搜集到的资料信息进行组织和加工处理，或者对原有假设进行检验、得出结论，或者提出解决问题的初步方案，或者对各种可能的问题解决方案进行比较后选择一个最佳的答案。为了帮助学生更深入地了解和认知城市商业化，我们请到了成都市设计院的王磊主任给学生们做了一个青龙场改造的案例分享。王主任分享了案例中商业元素与文化元素结合的思考，同学们也踊跃提问，在真实的商业化案例中进行深入探究。

王磊主任的讲座

（6）在最后一个部分，学生分小组进行研究文章写作。在写作过程中，学生运用自己收集的数据和前期的研究形成自己的观点并回答问题。

论文的评估标准如下：

Task Achievement	The essay had a clear thesis statement, expressed in the opening paragraph. The whole essay is focused on the central idea expressed in the thesis statement, while fully exploring multiple aspects of the topic.
Content	Main ideas are comprehensively supported with ample, specific, relevant evidence and examples.
Organization	The essay is well organized and follows the essay style. Ideas are very effectively organized with variety linking devices within and between paragraphs. The format is clear and appropriate. Well planned and executed.
Sentence Structure	A very wide range of structures are effectively used. Writing is accurate. Errors are minor and do not hinder communication.
Vocabulary	Appropriate and effective use of a very wide range of general and specialist vocabulary. No errors in spelling.
Reference	Appropriate resource selection and consistent citation and reference list.

三、课程反思

本次研学活动整体来说是成功的。本课程采取沉浸式学习的方式,培养学生的批判思维能力与研究学习能力。

在课程组织过程中,学生能够积极主动地学习,探究式学习充分调动了学生的内在积极性。从后期的写作产出中也能看到学生能够进行自主研究学习。

前期的调研组织可以更加精细,前期的规划调研需要专家的引领,在数据收集方面也需要给学生更多的支持,尤其是如何科学地收集数据和观察,以及如何对数据进行有效性评估。

后期的文章写作可以成为持续一个整学期的项目,在初稿以后可以写出二稿和终稿。学生在教师的指导下不断进步与反思,能更好地培养其元认知能力。

四、作业展示

The Success of China Lane: History, Architecture, Commerce

Abstract

China Lane, a prolonged and famous attraction in Chengdu, has been developed for several decades. During our group's field trip, we paid attention to China Lane's commercial transformation. In this report, we are going to analyze how China Lane becomes so prosperous in three aspects: its history and culture, architecture building style, and its commerce.

Background and History

After the Manchurians entered the Central Plains, part of the Qing army moved into Sichuan and Sichuan became a gathering place for the nobles of eight Banners and the children of Shaocheng.

After the Revolution of 1911, Zhao Erfeng, the governor of the Qing Dynasty, surrendered the government power and dismantled the walls of Shaocheng. Some dignitaries came here to build mansions and civilian houses. Yu Youren, Tian Songyao, Li Jianyu, Yang Sen, and Liu Wenhui successively settled here.

In 1948, in an urban survey, it was said that the staff at that time marked the wider lanes as "wide lane", and the narrower one as "narrow lane".

Even though modern "China Lane has been dramatically reformed" (starting from Zhijishi Street in the north, reaching Jinhe Street in the south, reaching Changshun Street in the east, and including Tongren Road in the west), it still contains a lot of historical and cultural atmosphere when approaching the modern Broad and Narrow Alley, such as Kai Lu, Demen Renli, brick cultural walls, and small houses. Besides necessary decorative buildings, many shops also contain rich historical and cultural atmosphere in the Broad and Narrow Alley, such as teahouses in quadrangle courtyard, plainclothes shops in ancient style, and teahouses with a stage to perform the opera. The tourists can enjoy the delicious food in the alley and perceive the history of Sichuan.

Walking into Zhijishi Street, one will submerge in the shade of trees which set off old-style residential buildings. The street is quiet but full of busy private stores, including restaurants and even the traditional Chinese instrument club. There are no modern high-rises and manufacture noise, all of which are suitable for the old street on sunny Wednesday afternoon.

China Lane is a unique symbol of Northern Hutong Culture in the southern towns. In other words, it is the representative of combining courtyard culture and Hutong culture. It can be traced back to the Qing Dynasty when the Broad Alley was called Xingren Hutong, and Narrow Alley used to be Taiping Hutong.

Yang Jianying, the designer of China Lane, once said the key to constructing China Lane is not simply pursuing cultural symbols and appearance of traditional buildings, but to discover, extract, and create contemporary and future vitality of culture and industry in the shell of historical buildings, to create a root that can absorb the nutrients of the present and the future, to create a body that can continue to blossom and flourish. Naturally, cultures shape the buildings. But sometimes cultures live in the buildings at the same time. As a result, architecture can be regarded as a pattern of original culture or a display of local customs. More importantly, the cores can be diverse in the same style of buildings. Take Starbucks as an example. Although it is true that some foreign brands may trigger cultural conflicts with the local one, Starbucks actually reaches the balance between American culture and traditional Chinese culture. Before our group members went deep into the alleys, we carried some stereotypes and biases towards cultural diversity. We used to think two completely different cultures cannot co-exist in one place, for they have many differences that would block cultural assimilation. However, what presented on these streets surprise us by showing how western and eastern features can perfectly be merged. Because of this, China Lane attracts tourists from different backgrounds to appreciate the natural fusion of different cultures.

In terms of the road constructions, all the alleys are generally planned into the fish spin model, in which the alleys were paved with aged bricks and stones, providing as a retro style.

The house of Debauve et Gal has a Chinese style roof and a western style

Roman column, which props up the balcony on the second floor. It is a surprise to see this building in a Chinese historical site.

Another example is No. 11 Residence in the China Lane, which belonged to those who returned from abroad, and the house was decorated with a western style archway.

Commercial Operation of China Lane

Under the background of developing a "Leisure City," Chengdu government launched the renovation project of the historical and cultural China Lane in 2003. The government determined to form a complex commercial block with strong local characteristics and the cultural atmosphere of Bashu. The government has invested more than 630 million Yuan to support this project. Finally, in 2008, the reconstruction project of China Lane was completed and officially opened on June 14.

With the development of economy, many commercial streets arose all over the country, but many of them failed to thrive. However, the development of China Lane is very successful: the integration of "government, company, and merchant" protects China Lane's commercial profit, which is government operating environment, enterprises operating market, and people operating culture.

Many regular old shops in the Broad and Narrow Alley have been open since 6 years ago. In addition to the "estate", there are also mobile commerce settings. These mobile shops are not only small mobile sales points, but also small cultural display windows. Visitors are quickly drawn to China Lane through moving shops at the entrance.

There are also some music festivals and small concerts on the street. The

"Street Music Season" has also been held in China Lane. "Numerous events and performances can be found in the China Lane", and it is these intangible cultural events that inspire people's memories of Chengdu and attract visitors from outside. China Lane also has a wine shop. In addition to the genuine plum wine, foreign wine and beer are sold.

Also, stores with "foreign coffee culture" such as Starbucks and One Coffee are popular among tourists. However, in particular, these coffee shops decorated themselves in Chinese Style. Starbucks has retained the architectural form of residential style in western Sichuan.

China Lane achieved an excellent blend of different cultures. In terms of preserving all the original objects and architecture, China Lane activates and inherits the culture through commercial models.

Conclusion

From those aspects above, we can say that the success of China Lane is attributed to its architecture, history, combing style, and commercial transformation.

采取行动篇

课案十三

项目化学习之"财商与决策"

课程设计教师:

钟佩好

双语经济学教师

执教 IB/AP 经济

五年新加坡留学经历

获 TKT 英语能力证书;获 CMFAS 金融管理执照,曾任职于世界五百强英国保诚公司;教学及竞赛经验丰富,NEC 全美经济学挑战赛优秀教练员

内容:

一、课程背景

二、课程内容

三、课后作业

四、课后反思

一、课程背景

2008 年金融危机以后,美国把儿童财商教育提到了国家战略高度,他们认为每一位小公民从小就应该接受财商教育,具备良好的财经素养,这样今后才能更好地实现财务自由和经济独立,家庭经济运行良好才能让整个国家的经济处于良性运转状态。

芬兰在教育方面被许多教育界专家视为"全人教育的范本"。尤其在经济与财商知识学习方面，他们采用"我与城市"为主题，让孩子们扮演各种社会角色。例如，将一个房子模拟成一座微型城市，这座城市里有企业、商店、银行和公共服务机构等。孩子们进入"微城市"前要先上 10 节课，课程内容主题包括经济、社会、工作和创业等，旨在让学生直观地体会到什么是经济、什么是企业、工作是什么、如何找工作、为什么要交税、银行存在的意义等。

除了发达国家把财商教育列入中小学课程外，当前我国一些经济发达的地区也逐渐将财商教育纳入了课程体系之中，在一些国际学校或学校的国际部，经济、商管、会计等相关学科更是列为学生的必选科目之一。但是这样的课程覆盖广度还远远不够，许多学生依然没有很好的机会或渠道在初高中阶段学习与经济财商相关的课程。从长期发展的角度来看，提高中学生的经济与财商素养，对国家的经济发展有积极的推动作用。

二、课程内容

本次有关"财商与决策"的项目式学习一共有十二节课，最终的任务是让每个小组选择一个企业类型并开启自己的创业模式，在此过程中小组成员需要了解消费者行为和心理，学会分析市场，完成企业计划，搭建管理框架，计算成本与利润，应用营销组合策略。在第一个"知识储备"模块，我们安排了十节课，之所以花费一半多的课时来进行知识讲解，主要是由于这部分内容是高一学生在以往的学习经历中完全没有接触过的领域。

第一课，学生了解经济学基本概念，对经济学有一定的学术认知，发现经济学与生活常识的区别与共通性，能联系生活实际将理论应用到生活案例中。教师提前布置课堂，在课桌上随机放置饮料、饼干和糖果。学生进入课堂之后，根据自己的喜好选择入座，有些同学得到了桌子上的随机礼物，而有些同学则没有。教师邀请其中一位同学分享为什么选择了有饮料的座位。通过这个破冰活动，教师引入本堂课的主要内容。

第二课，教师依然通过课堂活动引入经济学的知识点。通过冰咖啡实验让学生了解收入支出在产品市场和要素市场之间是如何流通的，从而掌握供给和需求的概念，以及哪些因素会影响消费者需求。学生还会在这一课中学习如何借助重要的模型与图表来演示问题及其变化。

第三课，教师展示不同的市场结构，让学生通过观察生活中可见的商品市场或企业来了解不同市场结构的特点。

不同的市场结构

教师引入SWOT矩阵分析法，将市场结构的优势、劣势、机会和挑战更全面地通过SWOT工具来展示。介绍这一分析方法的目的是帮助学生在选择了创业公司类型之后对公司的各种环境因素，包括外部因素和内部因素进行客观分析和预设，并学会将调查得出的各种因素根据轻重缓急或影响程度等方式排序，构造SWOT矩阵。这一思维方式也能帮助学生在处理日常事务时更有条理和逻辑，成为一个更理性的决策者。

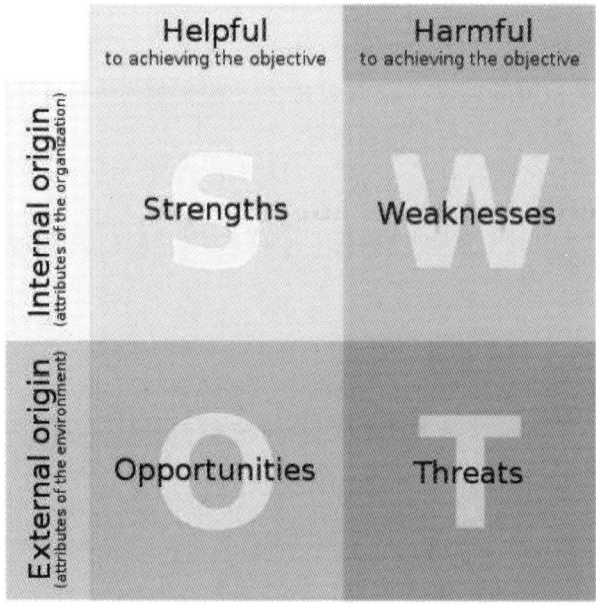

SWOT 矩阵分析法

第四课，课程内容正式从经济学通识进入商学基础的学习。在介绍了企业计划书和企业人员角色之后，学生自愿组队，形成8~10人一组的团队。组内初步确定团队内的人员角色，并通过队内选举的方式选出队长。队长将抽选出自己小组将要启动的创业类型。为了降低难度并尽可能地贴近学生生活，笔者将行业类型的范围缩小至咖啡店、餐馆、服装店、影院和酒店。各小组需要初步拟定计划书大纲，其中需涵盖商业计划书的几大基本要素，如商业计划目标、人员角色、创业过程中的步骤等，为后期查资料做足准备。

第五课，细化商业计划书。小组根据自己的行业类型查资料或做调查，分析需要考虑的商业因素。一些常见的商业因素如下：

- Business idea
- Finance
- Human resource
- Entrepreneurial skills
- Fixed assets
- Suppliers

- Customers
- Marketing
- Legalities

每组成员需要从本堂课开始围坐在一起,展开实时讨论,调查实际案例中出现的商业因素和风险因素。教师可提供一些资料和模板,如 Uber 公司的 Model Canvas,给学生一些思路和启发。

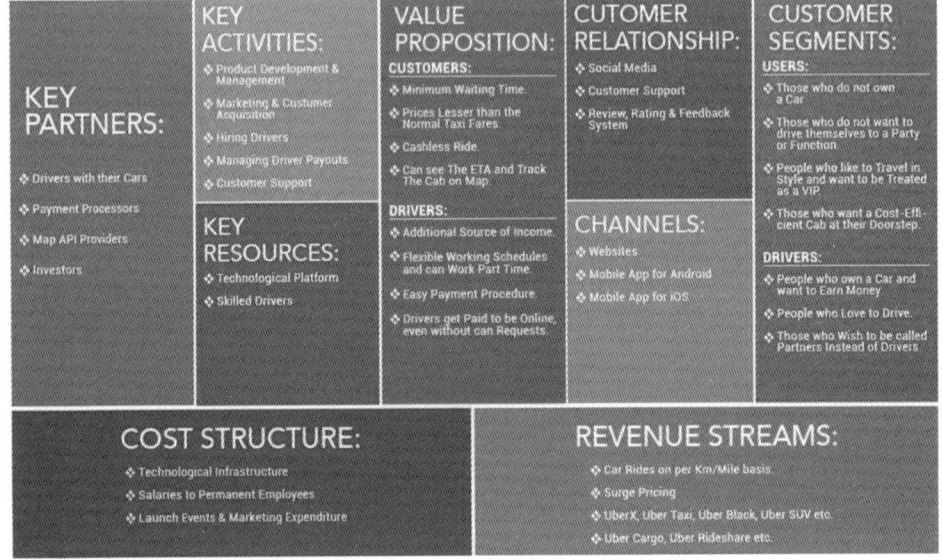

Uber 公司的 Model Canvas

小组还需要在当下的经济情况和市场环境下,预设自己在经营期间会遇到的问题。如新冠肺炎疫情可能带来的运营冲击,并讨论和分享相应的对策。这其实也是目前中小企业面临的巨大挑战。最后,教师再补充介绍企业会面临的常规问题,小组成员可以据此补充和完善自己的计划。

第六课,组织与管理。各小组已确定组内人员的角色及分工,小组人员的角色可有一次变动的机会。因为在实践操作和讨论中,在学生对职位角色有了更深入的了解之后,可能会发现自己的性格和能力与目前的职位不太匹配,例如,担任会计的学生认识到自己不能很好地胜任账目记录以及资产负债的计算工作。

第七课，本堂课的主要内容是完成一个角色扮演（Role-play）活动。各小组展示家庭作业"管理架构图"，组长分别介绍员工角色和职能。各小组模拟董事会或团队会议时的场景。小组还需要根据自己从事的行业类型形成自己的组织文化。

第八课，成本与利润。学生了解成本的类型并掌握基本的成本收益计算法。小组分析可能会影响企业利润的因素，理解盈亏分析的重要性。教师要求小组根据自己抽选的行业类型，将成本从高到低排序。具体要求如下：

Further research work—make a list of cost

According to the "cost ranking" result from class activity, each group based on their own business do a further research about cost information of one business.

第九课，营销组合策略。新店选址对初创企业来讲是非常重要的决策之一，了解地点分布的类型与具体选址需要考虑多方面的因素。学生将选址大范围定在成都市，初步拟定选址计划，完成以下活动设计：

"Where to locate my business in Chengdu?"

Case analysis

Assume your new business will start in the city of Chengdu. Choose your location and provide reasons why you want to distribute your coffee shop/restaurant/clothing store/cinema/hotel there. Your reasons must contain evidence such as survey, data and relevant information.

第十课，课程进入尾声也开启了一个重要的环节——给产品定价。学生了解价格战略方案及促销战略方案，并考虑线上平台可能会给自己的实体店带来的冲击。尤其像咖啡店、餐馆和服装这类中小型企业，更应该了解竞争者的优势和劣势，这样才能使一个新的企业更好地在市场中存活下来。

三、课后作业

结束了充满挑战的十节课后，在学生正式汇报成果之前，教师还分享了自己在大学期间完成的一份商业计划，这是与本次财商与决策课程内容非常相似的一个项目。分享该商业计划的首要目的是为学生再梳理一遍核心知识点、关键内容和整体结构；其次教师还想跟学生分享自己在完成这项任务的过程中面临的困难，比如，当小组成员之间意见不统一甚至有矛盾的时候，成员们是采取什么方法来化解的。

学生展示环节安排了两节课，一共 10 组，每组分别上台介绍自己的企业项目、企业名称及各成员的角色和职能。由于人数众多，每组选择 4 位同学为代表上台讲解。下面是咖啡店和餐馆两个小组的商业创意。

学生展示环节

咖啡店

咖啡店小组把营销重点放在了促销手段上。他们选择了线下销售点展示的方法，这很符合当下流行的"地摊经济"文化，能精准定位爱喝咖啡的年轻消费者，将文化与营销有效结合。同时他们还参考了一些成功的商业品牌，如星巴克、瑞幸等在初创阶段所采用的策略，他们如何缩减成本，选择不同价位的咖啡机和咖啡豆是否会对企业的收益带来很大影响。根据真实的商业案例，小组成员通过计算成本收益，结合自身的咖啡厅定位，向我们传达了一套减少成本的方案：打造社区型咖啡店，主打外带的购买方式，选择无座位空间的小区域门店，从而减少房租的固定成本和员工工资的可变成本。随着成本的降低，迷你社区型咖啡店有充足的降价空间，便有机会与同类商品打一场价格战。

餐馆

新冠肺炎疫情期间不少小型餐馆倒闭，这也给抽到餐馆的初创团队带来了额外的难度。令人欣喜的是，该小组充分考虑到疫情期间饮食安全和疾病传播的问题，推行半加工食品，且要确保食物的密封性和安全性。

这个创业想法非常有意思，但紧接着这个小组的同学客观地分析了他们面临的困难：第一个问题是包装成本高。要做到消毒规范且真空包装无污染，在产品包装上可能要花费很高的成本甚至导致资源浪费，造成额外的成本和环境污染，违背了可持续发展的原则。第二个问题是如何将食物的口味更好地传递给顾客。半加工的食品在安全和口味上往往要做一些权衡取舍，完好无损的包装可能会牺牲食物本身的美味，这也涉及如何引导顾客正确再加工，因为顾客操作不当也会导致风味流失。餐馆小组的讲解体现出辩证的思维模式，根据自己提出的想法结合SWOT策略，实现多维度分析。

四、课后反思

1. 背景、情景、结构化的知识

本次融合创新课程突显了融合的特点，课程内容集合了经济、商管、市场、金融等多个领域的知识。由于内容广度和跨度都较大，很难建立起章节之间的联系，导致后期知识的迁移和运用难以在演讲报告中体现出来。这也是一些小组成员在展示环节中显得困惑的原因。比如，在第二节课学生学习影响消费者需求的非价格因素时，我们介绍了五个影响因素：

（1）消费者数量。

（2）收入水平。

（3）相关产品的价格（包含互为补足的商品和互为替代的商品）。

（4）商品未来的价格变化。

（5）直接税。

单看这五个因素是比较抽象的，但讲清楚了这些知识点及其学术定义，学生是否就能很好地将这些概念和原理与实际生活中的例子建立联系呢？就个人来讲，除了基本的知识，笔者还会补充一些实际的例子，微观层面上就以日常生活中的事例举例，宏观上可以联系时事要闻，提供一个具体的情景或背景让学生更好地去假设和推理。在备课时，教师还要注意准确把握内容的难度和深度，真正做到寓教于乐，让学生在轻松的课堂氛围中学习。

2. 教学流程

首先，让学生清晰地知道在这堂课、这个项目中要学什么是非常重要的。在第一节课中，笔者介绍了任务目的和期望，让学生做到心中有数，这样在学习时既不会太迷茫也不会太敷衍。

其次，每节课的学习目标（Learning Objectives）会更细致地说明本节课的学习内容，学生在复习时也可以就关键的目标内容来进行复习整理。

最后，笔者认为一节课最重要的部分是扼要复述（Recap）环节，如果能在课程结束之前带着同学们把当堂课的重点内容再梳理一遍，同学们能更好地掌握和总结所学知识。

3. 教学活动

在课堂活动中，对于没有直接参与活动的同学来讲，他们的学习体验感会差一点。比如，在模拟商业会谈的活动中，笔者采取的是小组选派成员进行展示，有部分英语口语不那么好的孩子可能会有所胆怯而选择退缩，那么这个活动给他带来的影响是非常小的。如果课程时间允许，可以单独用一节课来模拟会谈，教师可以给小组所有成员都安排好任务并录像。英语口语表达能力不那么强的同学可以担任秘书一职，做好会议记录。总而言之，每位同学都要在商业会谈中发挥自己的价值，不做活动的旁观者。

课案十四

经济学思维

课程设计教师：
吴诗然
英国杜伦大学金融学硕士
AP 经济学执教资质认证
曾在伦敦公立中学进行 A-Level/GCSE 经济学教学

内容：
一、教学对象
二、教学内容
三、教学方法
四、课程目标
五、教学设计——第一课时
六、教学设计——第二课时
七、教学设计——第三课时

一、教学对象

本课程适用对象为 K12 中学阶段 10—12 年级学生。本课程教学策略设计以活动启发和课堂讨论为主，对学生的社会经验、知觉、注意和思维有一定要求。高一及以上年级的学生已经具备了一定的社会生活常识；知觉的有意性和目的性有了较大提高，能自觉地根据教学要求感知有关事物；抽象思维也开始由"经验型"向"理论型"转化。考虑到学生对于经济案例和概念的理解有局限，教学设计中应考虑概念普及的环节。

二、教学内容

本课程作为经济学导入课程，重点介绍经济学要解决的基本问题。在知识层面，学生需掌握基本经济学问题中所涉及的基础概念和主要矛盾。课程难点在于应用经济学思维解读经济学现象，并进一步思考如何解决经济学中的核心矛盾。

三、教学方法

本课程主要采用活动启发法、分析讲授法、情景讨论法。

四、课程目标

1. 知识目标
（1）理解经济学含义及其要解决的基本问题。
（2）理解风险、选择、信息、机会成本的含义。
（3）理解资源和需求的定义。
（4）了解"理性经济人"假设。
2. 能力目标
（1）能将经济学思维应用至个人和组织决策中，并能从学科角度解读小至个人层面、大到国家层面的决策。
（2）通过课堂实践，培养学生从感性认识到理性分析、透过现象分析本质的思考力和逻辑思维能力。
（3）通过课堂主题讨论，培养学生的批判性思维。
3. 情感、态度与价值观目标
（1）通过参与式学习引导学生探索直接环境以外的世界，关注全球重大议题（如环保节能），提升全球胜任力。
（2）通过主题引领和讨论，引导学生以"国家建设者"的身份去思考国家发展。

五、教学设计——第一课时

1. 课堂导入：破冰游戏

教师在简单询问学生眼中的经济学后开始破冰游戏。

（1）游戏准备：准备 4 份不同的小奖品，如零食、便笺纸等。

（2）游戏机制：邀请 4 位游戏志愿者，按照举手的顺序分别编号 1、2、3、4 号，请 4 位志愿者依次从 4 份奖品中任意挑选一份"免费的礼物"。其中 3 号同学需要"盲选"（即只能说左手或右手，在决定以前教师可以将手背在后面任意换手）。

2. 分析讲授：游戏解读和延伸

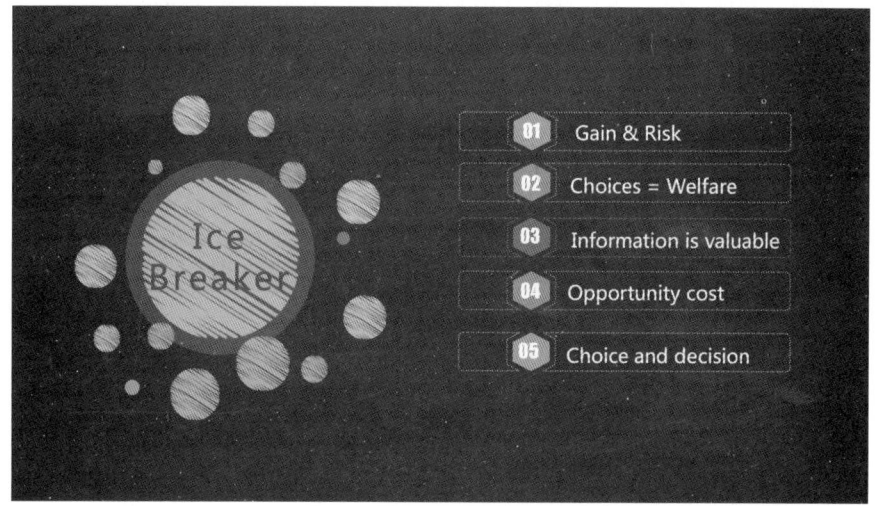

（1）采访未参加游戏的同学为什么没有举手参与这个"有百利而无一害"的游戏，引导学生关注"风险"是一种可能性与不确定性，不同于"危险"。因而"风险"并不是一个负面的概念，且收益与风险往往是成正比的。

（2）采访 4 号同学，如果他（她）可以第一个选礼物会不会做出不一样的选择或有不一样的感受，引导学生讨论"拥有选择"的好处。在学生从个人层面讨论了生活中的选择后，教师可引导学生关注和探讨国际贸易带来的选择层面的福利。

（3）采访 3 号同学，如果他（她）能看着选礼物会不会有不一样的选择或感受，引导学生关注决策中信息充分的重要性。教师可引导学生关注"股市内幕交易"的话题和互联网如何在信息层面帮助了个人和组织的决策（如求职）。

（4）采访所有游戏志愿者，询问他们是否觉得自己今天获得的奖品是免费的，引出"机会成本"的概念，并区分"机会成本"与"会计成本"，从而引出"经济学思维"与"金融学思维"的差异，并明确经济学是研究选择和决策的学科。

（5）经济学解决的基本问题——稀缺性（Scarcity）。通过提问引发学生思考游戏中"机会成本"产生的原因——奖品的稀缺性，进而一般化为经济学解决的稀缺性问题，即资源是有限的，欲望是无限的。

> **The Basic Economic Problem**
>
> Resources are scarce but wants are infinite, meaning choices have to be made over how to allocate scarce resources efficiently.

3. 课堂讨论

讨论问题：How to alleviate the basic economic problem based on its definition?

引导思路：由讨论引导学生关注"Resources"和"Wants"这两个关键概念。

4. 课后思考作业

（1）What do we need to produce bread?

（2）What is the difference between wants and needs?

（3）What is Consumerism?

六、教学设计——第二课时

1. 课堂导入：问题思考
(1) What do we need to produce bread?
(2) What is the difference between wants and needs?
2. 概念讲解

The definition of "Resources", "Needs" and "Wants".

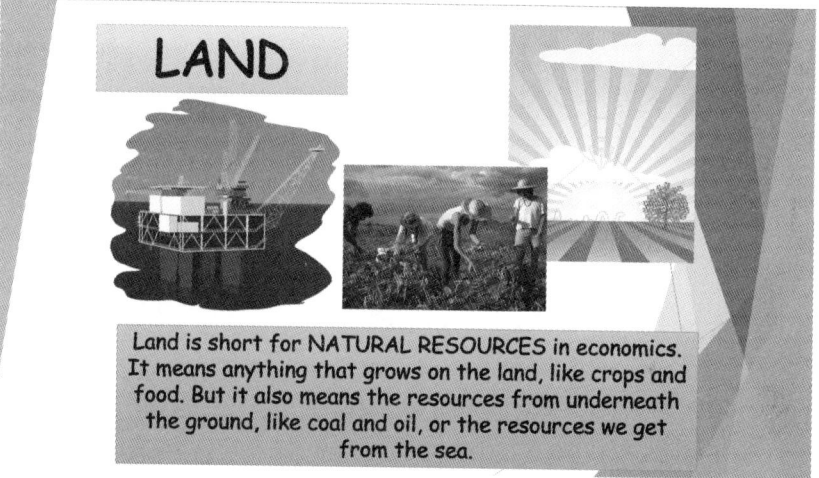

Land is short for NATURAL RESOURCES in economics. It means anything that grows on the land, like crops and food. But it also means the resources from underneath the ground, like coal and oil, or the resources we get from the sea.

Needs VS. Wants

Needs: Needs refer to the minimum necessary in order to survive as a human being. Examples include food, water, warmth, clothing, shelter.

Wants: Wants refer to desires for the consumption of goods and services. Examples include cars, JD shoes, chocolate.

3. 课堂讨论

讨论问题：How to alleviate the basic economic problem based on its definition?

引导思路：

The work on resources and wants including：

（1）The inter-temporal allocation of resources—Stricter Export Controls on China's Rare Earth.

（2）The improvement of productivity—education, science, technology and innovation.

（3）The criticism of consumerism. (Video clip: What is Consumerism?)

（4）The concept of carbon neutrality.

4. 课后思考作业

Focus on a decision you have made recently and think about how you made the decision, or the process you have gone through when you were making the decision.

七、教学设计——第三课时

1. 课堂导入：问题思考

Who are making decisions in economy? What are the decisions they have made?

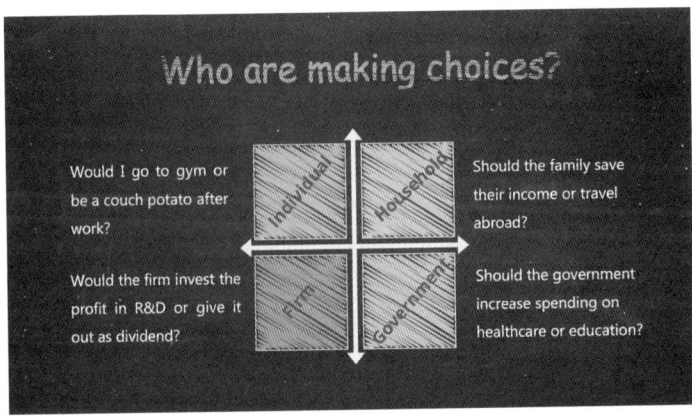

2. 概念讲解

(1) The economic agents and the mechanism of decision-making process.

(2) The economic rationality assumption in Neoclassical Economics.

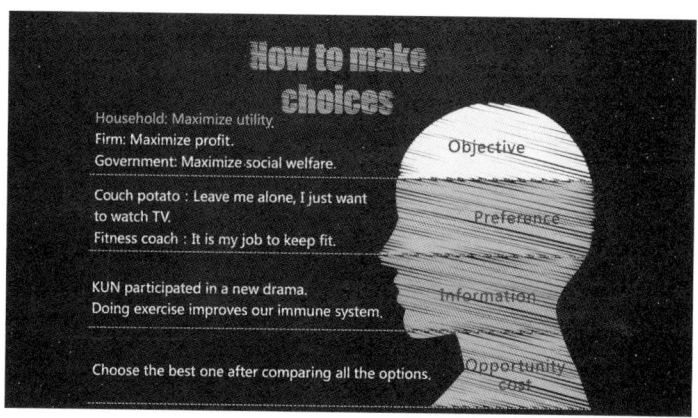

3. 课堂讨论

(1) Do you agree with the "economic rationality assumptions"?

(2) How scarce resources are allocated in each of the case below?

COVID-19 vaccination: government.

Football player: free market (price mechanism).

Internet celebrity restaurant: first come, first served.

4. 课后思考

Evaluate whether the resource allocation mechanism can help alleviate the basic economic problem in each case above.